SMASHING
MINDSET
TRAIN YOUR BRAIN TO
REBOOT RECHARGE REINVENT
YOUR LIFE

Second edition, revised and updated from the 1st edition, *MiGGi Matters:
How to train the brain to manage stress and trim the body*. First published
in the U.S. 2016. Thrive Publishing.

ISBN: 978-0-9990997-0-4(paperback)
ISBN: 978-0-9990997-1-1(ebook)

Library of Congress Control Number: 2017913924

Cover design and 2nd edition layout by Jenny Cowan
Illustrations by Jane Mjolsness
Printed in Australia and the U.S.A.

THRIVE Publishing
A Division of PowerDynamics Publishing, Inc.
San Francisco, California **www.thrivebooks.com**

SMASHING MINDSET

TRAIN YOUR BRAIN TO
REBOOT RECHARGE REINVENT
YOUR LIFE

Dr. Selena E. Bartlett.
Neuroscientist

THRIVE
PUBLISHING

San Francisco, California

This book is dedicated to

Francesca (1968-2006)
A brain lost to save others

CONTENTS

AUTHOR'S NOTE

I began writing this book in 2013, when my son, James, told me, "If you are able to make a difference, you should."

I decided to become a neuroscientist some twenty-five years ago, ignited by the unnecessary suffering endured by my sister Francesca. Although mental illness can be as painful and life changing as cancer or heart disease, Francesca found far less compassion than those suffering from a chronic physical disease. In my experience, people hospitalized with mental health problems rarely receive flowers. I could not understand why her illness had to lead to additional pain for her, our family, and, in a larger sense, society as a whole.

I came to feel it resulted from a general lack of understanding as to how the brain works. You would never say to someone with cancer, "Get over it." Yet that's just what some people seemed to feel Francesca should do—as if she had some control over her illness.

And yet, most of us can control some of what our brain does. Neuroscience and brain imaging are revolutionizing our capacity to see inside the brain. It has slowly become more accepted that the brain, no matter one's age, has an extraordinary capacity for change.

My search to learn about the brain started in Brisbane, Queensland, Australia, guided by my professional experience as a pharmacist and then as a medically trained neuroscientist. This book is a result of scientific research in my own lab, the research of hundreds of other people, and my own experience.

It is not a traditional neuroscience text. I have included all source material for this book in a section titled "Source Notes". I do not use footnotes because this is not an academic book but If you want to read in more detail about the subject matter, you can use the numbers in the text to find articles, websites, and more detailed information in the "Source Notes" section. Written for the average person, specifically around issues concerning addiction, diet, and exercise, the book reflects what I learned in my own quest for a healthier life, and from interviewing real people, outside my lab, who were crying out for a simple user's manual for the brain.

It's almost impossible to change your brain without understanding how it works. I am grateful to be delivering the message that transformed my brain, my body, and my life.

INTRODUCTION

You can beat the genetic lottery.

No matter who you are, where you were born, or how you grew up, you have one thing in common with everyone else: You started life with a ticket in the genetic lottery. Some people definitely hold winning tickets: born into the arms of two loving, stable parents, in a safe country, with no worries about food or shelter or access to a good education.

Many others, of course, start life in a far less promising way — carrying the genes of unstable, unhealthy, or unloving parents, born into a world of poverty, prejudice, lack of opportunity. For many, this random beginning becomes the middle and end of their life story as well. And yes, our genes, our environment, and our experiences do shape who we are — but they don't have to define who we become.

Picture rolling a rock down a hill. It will keep going until something stops it, right? That's your **mindset: your habitual, unconscious ways of living and thinking**. Like that rock, your mindset keeps you eating too much, or believing you're unworthy of love, or dwelling on past pain, until something causes it to change. Or rather, until something causes you to change your mindset.

You might believe that you can alter the effects of your environment but are stuck with your genes, and in one sense, you're right.

You'll always have those brown eyes or that curly hair. But just as you can use colored contacts or straighten your hair, you can overcome your family's predilection for, say, addictive behavior or gaining weight. You can replace the things that are holding you back with things that will move you forward.

How? **You have the power to change your mindset**: to let go of past ways of being and thinking and to shape your future. Think of people who were born into deprivation and yet succeeded in creating rich, healthy lives for themselves and their children. Think of people who overcame bad habits and lost weight or cut back on their drinking or got out there and got a better job. People we admire as resilient or strong simply have a drive or a mindset to succeed. You can develop one, too.

We can't change our ticket in the genetic lottery, but we can control what we do about it. It takes daily work and practice, but it gets easier. Consider this book a roadmap—a user's manual for taking charge of your life. Learn how your brain works; how to recognize the patterns that keep it locked up, repeating the past; and how to apply simple strategies to change it.

It's never too late to change your future by smashing your mindset.

SELENA'S STORY: How my brain made me fat and unhealthy

I remember the moment as if it were yesterday. I'd had a suspicion that I was gaining weight: There was the slow creep up in dress size, the changes in style and color—the unconscious leaning toward black, loose-fitting clothing instead of the colorful, more fitted outfits I'd once worn. Even then, I felt uncomfortable in almost everything I wore.

One morning, I got up my nerve and stepped on the scale. When I looked down, I started to cry. How did this happen? I was the heaviest I had ever been. Beyond that, I was unfit and unwell. I often felt as if my insides were caving in.

The truth is, my body was falling apart, and I was only forty-four years old. I'd spent the past fifteen years paying attention to everything else: maintaining a stressful career, raising two children and caring for my family, staying connected with extended family. I'd faced several traumatic events, such as the loss of my beautiful sister, as well. I often sat at my desk for up to *ten hours a day*, on some days for as many as seven hours straight. Instead of eating well, preparing meals with lots of vegetables and lean meats, I regularly ate fatty and sugary food, especially when I was stressed. And exercise? Forget about it.

I realized I'd become trapped in a vicious cycle: The less I moved, the less I wanted to move, and the sicker I became.

In my twenties and thirties, I'd struggled with my weight. In those days, like everyone else, I believed that it was a matter of taking in fewer calories and getting more exercise. And like many people,

I'd tried many diets, on which I briefly lost weight before gaining it back again, and sometimes more. As I hit my forties, age and hormones were added to the mix. Dismayed and defeated, I felt this was the way it was going to be from now on.

You would think, as a neuroscientist specializing in addiction, I would have known better. The truth is, I had it completely wrong. It was my brain telling me to eat and drink more, not my body. In order to understand why, I had to step off the scale and into my lab.

Changing your future by changing your brain

I began my journey as a neuroscientist because of my sister's struggle with mental health issues and, toward the end of her life, with obesity. I spent twenty years researching alcohol addiction—trying with a laser focus to develop medications to treat that addiction—and five more studying sugar addiction.

Initially, we ran the alcohol experiments using sugar as a control. Then we made an incredible discovery: that sugar changes the brain by releasing a neurochemical that activates the nicotinic receptors. As you can see from the name, these are the same receptors that nicotine binds to. Sugar, we discovered, is as addictive as alcohol and nicotine, one of the most addictive drugs in the world![1,2]

Although the treatments I discovered had just a small effect on alcohol addiction,[3,4] I learned something more valuable along the way. I learned the way the brain works.

In particular, I learned the way the brain reacts to stress.[5] **I was getting fatter because of stress.** Like most people, I was not dealing well with the low levels of continuous stress in my life. Stress had me turning to comfort foods, which tend to be high in fat and sugar, and sometimes to alcohol. It was stress-induced overeating and under-exercising that was wreaking havoc on my body. And my brain was driving it all.

The brain developed over eons of history, and the oldest parts of the brain, the emotion circuits, remain at the center of many of our actions.[6] That less evolved part of the brain locks in our unhealthy, unconscious habits. I was like most people: When I was worrying about an upcoming deadline or money or the kids, I was habitually— and unthinkingly—relieving the stress with food and alcohol.

Becoming more aware of the brain and what it does to the body because of stress is the first step in losing weight and staying fit.

In the last decade, neuroscience and brain imaging have accelerated our understanding of the brain and its functions.[7] It was long thought that after a certain age, the brain is fully formed or fixed, and that it is almost impossible to change it. This is why most people believe a cliché like "You can't teach an old dog new tricks." That belief is simply untrue. There is a limit on willpower, but there is no limit on brainpower—the potential for your brain to change and learn new, healthy habits.[8, 9]

I saw this for myself some years ago when a young and gifted professor was working in the lab next to mine. Through the wonders of technology, I got a glorious view of her test subjects' brains while they were exercising. Eventually, she was able to map the brain, one synapse at a time. Her elegant, painstaking research revealed that the synapses in the adult brain are not static after all.[11] They are actually changing all the time. If your synapses can change, your habits can change.

While we can do nothing about the past, we have the ability to change our future. With effort and practice, we can retrain our brains using the principles of *neuroplasticity*.[8-11]

Neuroplasticity [noor-oh-pla-stis-i-tee, noun]. The brain's ability to reorganize and change by forming new synapses, or neural connections, between the nervous system and the brain.

Neuro, as in the brain, and *plastic*, as in moldable, not fixed. Neuroplasticity refers to the capacity of your brain to make new connections. With daily practice, the brain can be taught to work differently. In other words, you can definitely teach an old dog new tricks!

I was writing about this — about teaching the brain to be resilient[12-15] — when I had a huge "Aha!" moment. I suddenly understood: **I was getting fatter because my stressed brain was controlling me, and not the other way around.**

With this new knowledge and an understanding of the principles of neuroplasticity, I realized that I could control how my brain responds to stress. In fact, I could teach it to work differently. **I really could change unconscious habits** that were making me unhappy, unhealthy, and overweight.

No one ever says, "I could overcome my broken ankle if I just tried hard enough." That would be ridiculous. But when we struggle to break a habit, or we resolve to eat healthier or go to the gym more often, and fail, we blame ourselves, don't we? We tell ourselves, "I'm lazy" or "I'm not trying hard enough."

> It is not about **WILLPOWER**.
> It is about **BRAINPOWER**.

In talking to people around the globe, whether it's the CEO of a multimillion-dollar company, a health professional, a teacher, a government official, a clerk or secretary or maid, I've found few people with even a basic understanding of how the brain works. They almost never know what happens in their brains when they are stressed, how it dictates their choices, and how that affects their health.

And yet, there are fascinating physiological reasons that you do what you do when you are upset or worried. Several popular TV shows have demonstrated that almost anyone can lose weight in the short term. Without understanding how the brain works, however, and changing what it is doing, most people cannot sustain that weight loss.

This book is *not* about dieting, because, in the long term, diets make us fatter and unhealthy.[16] It will tell you about the emotional part of your brain.[6] I call it MiGGi, because it contains the amygdala: and MiGGi is a term that is easier for everyone to relate to. My book will explain how that part of your brain works, especially when you are stressed—*why* you reach for those chips or cookies. I call it having a MiGGi moment, although it's really less than a second, too short for you to consider what you are doing. With this book, you'll learn how to teach your brain to pause after that millisecond reaction to stress—to take a second or two and give your brain time to stop, think, and make a rational response to what's upsetting you, instead of encouraging you to reach for food or drink. This book will help you train your brain to learn new, healthier habits.

Smashing Mindset is an interactive guide to engage and educate you about your brain and how it is affected by stress, sugar, high-fat foods, alcohol, and lack of exercise. It will show you how to use your brain to develop healthy habits instead.

The book is based on six simple principles that, when applied on a daily basis, train the brain to manage stress and trim the body.

THE 6 PRINCIPLES

PRINCIPLE 1: Get to know your brain
Introducing Scout, MiGGi, and Thinker, and why MiGGi matters most

PRINCIPLE 2: Become aware of how stress wires your brain for unhealthy habits
Identifying your particular stress reactions

PRINCIPLE 3: Retrain your brain to respond and not react to stress
Simple tools for recognizing when you are feeling stress; retraining your brain for healthier habits

PRINCIPLE 4: Manage stress by eating less sugar-containing and high-fat foods and beverages
Reducing sugar, fat, and alcohol intake; managing stress with healthy rewards

PRINCIPLE 5: Manage stress through movement
Improving cardio fitness; trimming your body; improving brain plasticity

PRINCIPLE 6: Love is the antidote to stress
Love is the key to good health, happiness, even survival

The first step in kick-starting your brain is …
getting to know yourself.

PRINCIPLE 1:

Get to know your brain

Introducing Scout, MiGGi, and Thinker,
and why MiGGi matters most

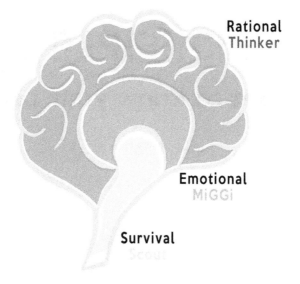

Rational
Thinker

Emotional
MiGGi

Survival
Scout

PRINCIPLE 1: Get to know your brain

JENNIFER'S STORY: Why change is so difficult

I knew her as the mother of one of my daughter's friends. That day, she was sitting beside me at a high school graduation. One of the students was absolutely endearing as she handed out awards, giggling at every opportunity and bubbling with life. Jennifer leaned over and whispered, "Remember when you felt so full of hope, when you couldn't wait for your life to unfold?" Just as I turned to her to say, "Yes!" she added, "Just wait until life smacks her in the face."

I was taken aback by her bitterness. She must have seen that in my face, because, in almost the same breath, she explained that when she was seven months pregnant with their second child, her husband had had an affair and left her. She nodded to the little girl sitting on her other side. Clearly, this had been a traumatic event—it had happened more than a decade ago!

I could feel her immense pain and suffering; I could see the dramatic effect it had had on her self-esteem, her confidence, and yes, her weight. She had been replaying these events in her mind for *years* — keeping alive her stress, which in turn contributed to her inability to let go. The way stress works in the brain keeps painful memories on instant replay.

KEY NOTE:
To make real change in our bodies and emotions, we need to understand the brain.

MEET THE THREE PARTS OF THE BRAIN:
Scout, MiGGi, and Thinker

Over the course of time, the brain evolved into a complex structure of highly interconnected wires or communication channels.[17] Due to the complexity of the brain, for the purposes of this book we will focus on only three main regions. Put simply, they can be considered the survival, emotional, and rational parts of our brain, and they are in constant communication.

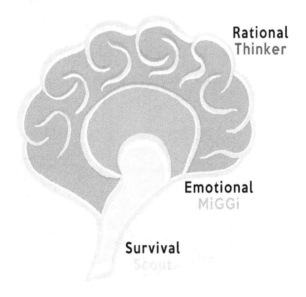

This is a simplified version of the complex structures of the brain: the survival part, the emotional part, and the thinking part.

MEET SCOUT: Your Survival Brain

The oldest part is the survival brain, which is thought to have first appeared in worms nearly five hundred million years ago.[17,18] It includes parts of the brain that are also found in reptiles, such as the brainstem and the cerebellum. Located just above the spinal cord, it is a relay station between the brain and the body.

I call this part of the brain Scout, because it is always on the lookout for threats and alerts the rest of the brain to imminent danger. Scout also controls the body's vital functions, such as heart rate, breathing, body temperature, balance, and the sleep-and-wake cycle.[19] Do you remember ever consciously thinking, "Okay, heart, time to beat"? No, because Scout does that for you.

Scout represents the survival part of the brain and is always scanning for physical threats.

MEET MIGGI: Your Emotional Brain

The limbic or emotional brain exerts a strong influence over our behavior.[6] It is where we record our memories of good and bad experiences. It is the part of the brain in which we feel emotions: fear, love, hate, anger, joy. It's also where we make judgments about ourselves and the world: When we decide whether something is safe to eat or a stranger is friend or foe, we are using this part of the brain. It was first seen in our ancestors about two hundred and fifty million years ago.[17, 20] The main structures are the amygdala, the nucleus *accumbens*, the hippocampus, and the hypothalamus.[6] I call it MiGGi, because the amygdala is so important.

The amygdala is a set of highly specialized nerve cells that transmit information to and from your brain to the rest of your body via the synapses, which are linked in neural pathways to create the central part of the nervous system. Assessing incoming stimuli, the amygdala is involved in our responses both to pleasure and to stress and fear.

Unfortunately for some of us, our emotional brains are hardwired to make fear, stress, and pain higher priorities than pleasure or happiness. That's because **the brain's main goal is our survival**.

MiGGi monster mode occurs when the brain is constantly scanning for physical threats. MiGGi koala mode occurs when we learn how to give the brain enough time to process pleasure and happiness.

Since MiGGi's main job is to keep us alive, when it gets stimuli from Scout it activates in mere milliseconds. Then it begins pumping out stress hormones, such as cortisol, and neurotransmitters, like noradrenaline. That causes the physical sensations—heart palpitations, sweaty palms, muscle tension—that initiate the famous fight-or-flight response, alerting the brain to get the body to either stop dead, fight, or run away. This allowed our primitive ancestors to quickly respond to immediate threats, like a woolly mammoth or a poisonous snake.[21]

Together, MiGGi and Scout are experts at finding threats and danger. That's why we tend to hold onto negative memories more effectively than positive memories: It ensures that we remember not to reach into a fire, for instance. In fact, most languages contain more negative words than positive words, because there's more adaptive value in being able to recognize, remember, and describe negative events.

The problem is, Scout and MiGGi still assume that any threat is a physical threat. And sometimes we do need to respond instantaneously, to a falling rock, say, or an oncoming car. But most of the time, we're facing something less immediate—the monthly bills, tomorrow's deadline or test, a first date. Those worries can activate MiGGi and Scout in the same way that spotting a woolly mammoth would, and then here come the stress hormones.

In excess and over a period of time, those stress hormones can harm our brain cells and its communication channels.[22] So the brain does something about it. Just as some parts of the brain respond to stress chemicals, like cortisol, others respond to pleasure or reward chemicals, such as the endorphins.[23-25] In an effort to keep itself alive, the brain balances the stress chemicals with feel-good chemicals.

Can you guess some of the things that activate the brain's reward or feel-good chemicals? Right! A hit of sugar,[26] a bite of fatty, greasy food,[27] a sip of alcohol,[28] a puff on a cigarette.[29]

These feel-good chemicals are situated in the parts of the limbic brain having to do with stress and fear (*amygdala*), pleasure or reward (the *ventral tegmental* area), motivation (*nucleus accumbens*), and feeding (*hypothalamus*). That explains why stress, reward, and eating are so intimately connected. It explains why, when you are upset, you end up eating sweets or potato chips or knocking back a whiskey or beer — habitual behavior that your brain has learned relieves your stress.

The great news is, **MiGGi doesn't care how it balances stress.** The brain can also get dopamine, serotonin, or endorphins from exercising,[30] interactions with other people,[31,32] and spending time in nature.[33,34] More on that later.

MEET THINKER: Your Rational Brain

A small neocortex was first seen in mammals about two hundred million years ago, but the rapid expansion into the neocortex, or rational brain, did not take place until about two and a half million years ago.[17] The neocortex of the human brain developed in parallel with changes in our diet, culture, technology, social relationships, and genes, and came into existence in Africa about two hundred thousand years ago. This is what enabled human cultures to develop. It is the site of human language, consciousness, abstract thought, and imagination. This part of the brain is rational and flexible and has an infinite capacity for learning. I call it Thinker.

Thinker is the coach, overseeing all the parts of the brain and getting them to work together. Thinker helps us resist temptation; this is what we mean by *impulse control,* which allows us to make decisions and to execute short- and long-range plans.[35] Otherwise, we would be sitting on the beach all day, or watching TV endlessly, or eating and drinking whatever we liked. You may be thinking, "Hey, that doesn't sound so bad." But you know we wouldn't get much done and would not be very healthy if we gave in to those impulses all the time.

Thinker mode occurs when Scout and MiGGi have enough time to scan and respond rather than react to stress.

Thinker operates best when we stop and think. That gives the brain the time it needs (mere seconds) to respond instead of to react—to realize that eating the whole bag of potato chips is not the best way to stay healthy. Thinker can control MiGGi, but it is exquisitely sensitive to stress from MiGGi. From an ancient survival perspective, reacting to immediate threats far outweighs our need to focus on our health, or plan for that important dinner party, or save for retirement. In real life, both Thinker and MiGGi are easily undermined by stress. Part of the problem is that the modern world, urged on by technology, information overload, and the rapid pace of change, has sped up, and our genes and brain have not sped up quickly enough to handle it. That, of course, just causes more stress.

KEY NOTE:
When we do not manage stress, stress manages us. It can feel as if we have a monster living inside us.

What happens to Thinker during a MiGGi moment

When we perceive a threat, the emotional part of the brain (MiGGi) will fire up in a millisecond and override the rational part (Thinker). That's fine when you're facing danger: If a truck is barreling down on you, you don't need to stop and think—you need to run. But this is also how our emotions can override our better judgment and hijack our thinking. Stress weakens the connections in a key region of the rational brain, the prefrontal cortex. When Thinker loses its ability to control MiGGi, we lose our ability to make good decisions, control impulses, and make plans. We choose immediate rewards over future ones.

When stress leads to a loss of self-control, we are shutting down Thinker and letting MiGGi take over.

| SCENARIO: Stressful situation | IF MiGGi RESPONDS: You choose between three extremes, fight or flight or freeze. |
| | IF THINKER RESPONDS: You make a rational, reasoned response. |

MACK'S STORY: A near-miss accident on replay

Mack is thirty-five years old. He and his wife, Susan, have been happily married for ten years and have a daughter, Charlotte. Mack is in middle management and has worked with the same company for five years. He has an hour-and-a-half commute on the freeway to work each day. Most of the time, he is a calm and reasonable person.

One morning, Mack was on his way to work, driving at the speed limit, listening to the radio. All of a sudden, a car driving ninety miles an hour narrowly cut him off. Mack slammed on his brakes, terrified. Just like in the movies, he saw his life flash before his eyes. Together, Scout and MiGGi worked brilliantly, activating Mack's reflexes to hit the brakes and keep him safe.

Once the terror receded, he felt shaken, upset, and very, very angry. Although there'd been no accident, Mack remained absolutely furious for days. Thinking about how he could have been killed, or maimed or paralyzed, or hit another car and hurt someone else, he kept mentally replaying the incident—over and over and over again. He couldn't stop thinking about finding the guy who'd cut him off and punching him in the face.

In other words, Mack continued to act and feel as if he were in danger. Without stopping MiGGi once it became clear that he was safe, MiGGi wound up controlling him. He was making himself sick. In the end, of course, only Mack suffered. The person who cut him off did not suffer at all.

> ## KEY NOTE:
> **In most cases, when MiGGi and Scout win out over Thinker, we lose.**

Your stressed-out brain

One of the ways MiGGi and Scout shut down Thinker in times of stress is by flooding the brain with hormones and chemicals. There's a good reason for this: to stop the rational part of the brain from considering too many possibilities and let MiGGi fire up a reflex response—the reason Mack slammed on the brakes instead of debating what to do. MiGGi's instantaneous charge of cortisol and noradrenaline saved Mack's life.

You could call that healthy stress. Worrying about money, your job, your kids, your health, or the state of the world causes unhealthy stress. Either way, cortisol will signal your reward center, getting you to seek whatever your brain has learned will make you feel calmer. We call this notion of stress and rewards the brain's scales of justice. On one side of the scale are the stress hormone, cortisol, and the neurotransmitters, such as noradrenaline. On the other side are the reward and pleasure chemicals, such as dopamine, serotonin, and endorphins. The goal is to keep everything in balance.

The Brain's Scales of Justice. The brain is balancing the toxic effects from chemicals like cortisol, which come from constant stress, with feel-good or reward chemicals, like dopamine and endorphins, which come from eating high-fat foods and sugar and drinking alcohol.

KEY NOTE:
If we don't handle stress, the brain finds a way to handle it for us.

ELIZABETH'S STORY: When stressing about work becomes a habit

Elizabeth is forty-four years old and has been the head of marketing for an international corporation for the last eight years. She leads a large team of people. Recently, the company has been facing unforeseen competition, and Elizabeth's team is under pressure to improve sales. With all this pressure, Elizabeth has been working longer hours. She can't remember the last time she went to the gym or got any exercise.

One Thursday morning, as she waited for her coffee to percolate, she opened her email, and her eyes went straight to a message from her boss. The work she'd thought was due in a week was due the next day. It was a complex, very important project; in fact, her promotion was riding on it. Whether she'd made a mistake or her boss had moved up the deadline wasn't important. Either way, the team could never be ready on time, and she would never get that promotion.

Elizabeth's stomach dropped, she felt short of breath, and her heart started racing. This tells you what was going on in her brain: MiGGi had fired up and Thinker had shut down. There was no way she could meet that deadline. She repeated this to herself like a terrible mantra, over and over again. There was no way they could meet that deadline.

By the time Elizabeth got to the office, however, everyone on her team had received another email, announcing that the deadline had been pushed back a week. Now they had more time to finish the project, not less. The feeling of relief was palpable, and the rest of the day went particularly well.

Even so, at the end of that day Elizabeth went home and had two or three glasses of wine. "I deserve that drink," she told herself. The immediate problem had abated, and yet she could not fully relax. Drinking each evening had become such a habit, whether she'd had a stressful day or not, it never occurred to her to go to the gym or a movie instead.

When MiGGi takes over and Thinker shuts down, the stress directly affects our bodies, making our hearts pound and our breathing quicken. When MiGGi drives us to reach for sugar or alcohol to make us feel better in the short term, Thinker loses sight of the long-term repercussions.

I used to be like Elizabeth: working too hard, relaxing too little, reaching too often for junk food, sometimes drinking too much. I, too, was getting fatter and unhealthier and unhappier. When I finally understood how MiGGi and Scout were taking control of my brain on a daily, even hourly, basis, it was the first step in getting out of my emotional brain and into my rational, thinking brain.

KEY NOTE:
Stress is what makes and keeps us fat and unhealthy.

PRINCIPLE 2:

Become aware of how stress wires your brain for unhealthy habits

Identifying your particular stress reactions

PRINCIPLE 2: Become aware of how stress wires your brain for unhealthy habits

Can you guess what is happening here?

You may have seen the viral videos featuring cats versus cucumbers.[36] Each video starts with a cat busy eating or otherwise distracted while someone places a cucumber behind it or outside its field of vision. When the cat turns around, it is inevitably so startled, it jumps into the air like a cartoon character. Maybe the cat thinks the cucumber is a snake.

As soon as it spots something it feels is dangerous, its immediate reaction is to escape. In terms of fight-or-flight, the cat's entire body goes into flight mode. This is the MiGGi stress and fear response in action — increased heart rate, shortened breath, muscles activated to *move*.

SCENARIO: Stressful situation	IF MiGGi RESPONDS: You choose between three extremes, fight or flight or freeze.
	IF THINKER RESPONDS: You make a rational, reasoned response to the source of stress.

Just as our bodies are unique, so are our brains and how they handle stress. This is why it is easier for some people to manage stress, reduce food intake, and exercise.

The way we *encounter stress*—a trigger or an event that makes us feel threatened, fearful, or upset—is the same. The trigger could be the look on someone's face, walking into a job interview, dealing with a screaming teenager, scanning an email from your boss. But we have two options for *dealing with stress:* We can react to it and move on, or we can react to it and then replay it, mentally and emotionally, over and over again. Whatever you do teaches the brain how to respond to that kind of trigger or event. Eventually, your response becomes automatic. This saves your brain a lot of energy and time.

When we replay events, however, no matter what solutions we may come up with, we cannot change what happened. Mack can re-experience his near-accident for a decade, Jennifer can look back on her divorce for the next twenty years, but what occurred will never be different. They know that—that is to say, Thinker knows it, but MiGGi keeps getting in the way. While MiGGi is managing things, they cannot set Thinker to the task of moving on.

As the renowned television producer Norman Lear, now ninety-three, puts it, describing his approach to life: "Over and next." I think we can all agree that there's nothing to be gained by going over things we cannot change—that it's best to focus on the present and the future. Letting go of the past and moving on, however, is more difficult for some people than for others.

> ## KEY NOTE:
> While every brain is capable
> of change, every brain is
> wired differently from stress.

Why is it harder for some people to manage stress?

Your brain is governed by your inherited genetic code *(genetics)* and the way it grows and is shaped over time by your environment and life experiences *(epigenetics)*.[37] While everyone's brain is capable of change, we experience different levels of stress over our lives. Some people have little stress early in life and are lucky to start adult life with a more resilient brain—that is, with a greater capacity to handle stress. Others have had a lifetime of stress, from childhood or even in the womb and onward.[38-40]

ANABEL'S STORY: Sugar as a baby

Anabel, fifty, recognizes that she has always used sugar to relieve stress. You could say that her mother trained her: She put chocolate syrup in Anabel's bottle when she was just six weeks old—quite young for a brain to start depending on the feel-good dopamine from that sugar hit. Perhaps it's no surprise to hear that Anabel had a stressful childhood, and even less surprising that she learned to handle stress with cakes, candy, and ice cream. This led to a lifetime of sugar consumption, usually at night, after a stressful day at work or when she was tired.

It didn't affect her weight too much until, in her mid-twenties, she was diagnosed with an autoimmune disease and given steroid medications. "My weight ballooned, and off I went—on this diet, that diet, the other diet. Over the years, I have become frustrated to the point of tears because I could not work out how to get rid of the weight."

Between the childhood stress and the sugar, we could have predicted that Anabel would have a weight problem as an adult.

Childhood stress affects the developing brain and is one of the leading causes of weight gain and obesity

Extensive research beginning early in the 1990s has directly linked childhood stress with many problems later in life. This research, since replicated around the world, is referred to as the Adverse Childhood Experiences (ACE) Study (www.acestudy.org).[41] Adverse childhood experiences have been shown to affect the development of the brain, thus increasing susceptibility for overeating, drinking alcohol, and/or experiencing depression and anxiety later in life.[42]

ACEs are one of today's greatest and most hidden public health crises. If we could reduce the number by just one event for every child and adolescent, we could reduce the economic and health burden on individuals, families, and communities. Because these unhealthy responses to early events often appear years or even decades later, however, they are rarely connected.

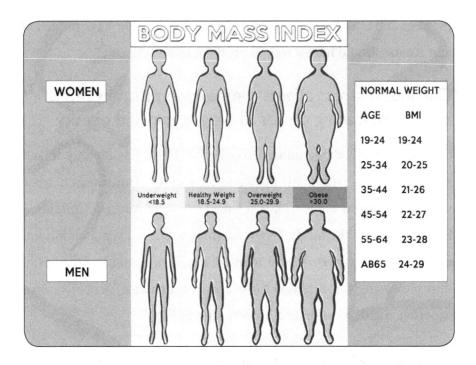

What the researchers were able to show is that the larger number of adverse childhood experiences a child has, the greater the chances that he or she will become overweight or obese. As the ACE score went up, so did the body mass index (BMI).[43]

The researchers stumbled upon this surprising observation while conducting a weight-loss study that began in 1985. Those who were most successful in losing weight all started to drop out of the study. When asked why, they usually said that they felt more attractive and didn't need to continue. It's likely that the memories and stress that had caused the weight gain resurfaced, and they didn't want to address any underlying issues or memories.

However, **it's all about how your brain works, not how you feel about whatever happened to you.** Ultimately, learning how to relieve your stress will be more helpful than digging into your past and reliving, and even understanding, your bad memories.

Over and over again, we leave the brain out of our thinking. Fitness centers, health-and-wellness training programs, diet and exercise books, and wearable monitoring devices all focus on the body. But when we pay attention to what's going on in the brain—to when and how often we have a MiGGi moment—we become aware of how stress is affecting what we do.

Situations that can trigger a stress response, or MiGGI moment:

- Coming upon something that frightens us, such as a spider or snake
- Going on a first date
- A job interview
- An upcoming test
- An important deadline
- Ongoing fear of losing your job
- Being cut off in traffic
- Your kids acting out
- Acute or chronic money troubles
- An unhappy relationship with your spouse or partner
- A separation or divorce
- Preparing for retirement

As you can see, these vary widely and are by no means equivalent experiences. MiGGi moments can be intense or mild, but they all affect your brain.

BETHANY'S STORY: Don't believe everything you think

Bethany is forty-two. She is divorced, has two children, works full time, and goes to a gym three times a week. When her ex-husband has the kids, she works out longer, as on this typical evening: After cranking on the exercise bike for an hour, she left the gym feeling good, proud of herself for working so hard, but on the way home, her mind began to wander. She started worrying about the bills she has to pay—how did there get to be so many? She wondered if her son, Billy, had been studying hard enough to get his grades up. Then she began thinking about Sally, the most difficult member of her team, and how lazy she is. Since Bethany didn't have to make dinner for the kids that night, she planned to work a little that evening and stopped to get some coffee— and then could not resist a large, buttery scone. Not a problem, she felt: "I can have it because I just worked out so hard." In other words, Bethany didn't feel she bought the scone without thinking.

What Bethany doesn't realize is that after focusing on all those stressful topics, she has reached for an unnecessary, high-calorie treat. That scone consists of close to five hundred calories, almost 50 percent fat and 25 percent sugar. Her brain wants that dopamine hit from the sugar and fat. Unless Bethany goes right back to the gym, those calories will show up in her body, particularly in her belly, and it will take a lot of cycling to burn them off.

"Am I having a MiGGi moment?"

Noticing when you are having a MiGGi moment allows you to feel how your brain reacts to stress before you are aware enough to do something to stop it. Without MiGGi awareness, it is nearly impossible to develop new, reasoned stress responses.

Write down three to six MiGGi moments you've experienced in the past week:

1. _____

2. _____

3. _____

4. _____

5. _____

6. _____

Keep a notepad near you, and every time you have one of these MiGGi moments, write it down. Do this every day for a week.

Now reflect on how you responded to those moments. What do you tend to do when you are having a MiGGi moment?

Examples:

+ Grab a donut, candy bar, or soda
+ Head to the vending machine for a snack
+ Consume a whole bag of chips before you realize it
+ Pour a glass of beer or wine
+ Yell at a coworker or your kids
+ Feel like you want to hit someone
+ Run away

To begin to trim your body, you should note how you cope with your MiGGi moments. Do you eat high-calorie food from the vending machine at work; drink two or more glasses of wine, beer, or alcohol at the end of a hard day; eat fries or ice cream late at night, or a candy bar in front of the television?

Write down what a MiGGi moment tends to lead you to do:

1. _____

2. _____

3. _____

4. _____

5. _____

6. _____

The brain is like a muscle, albeit one we use differently from a bicep or deltoid, and we can strengthen it at any age. Our brains are not fixed, as was once thought.[8]

KEY NOTE:
Just as, with effort and practice, the
brain can learn a new language or skill,
the brain can learn to respond
rather than react to stress.

PRINCIPLE 3:

Retrain your brain to respond and not react to stress

Simple tools for recognizing when you are feeling stress,
and retraining your brain for healthier habits

PRINCIPLE 3: Retrain your brain to respond and not react to stress

Your brain on a diet

The most primitive part of our brains evolved when little food was available and the main aim was to seek and store as much as possible. Our brains are hardwired toward consuming food, not moderating how much we eat. Furthermore, some of us have genes that make us susceptible to short-term gratification: Weak in impulse control, we find it impossible to think about the longer-term consequences of taking that extra piece of pie.

I think we all understand what we need to do to lose weight and keep that weight off: moderate our food intake, increase our physical activity, manage stress without food, seek treatment for depression if necessary. If losing weight makes us feel so much healthier and happier, why is it so hard to maintain?

When you start a diet, you feel purposeful and enthusiastic, ready to create a new relationship with food. However, the very word *diet* tells your brain it is going to be deprived. Moreover, the self-image you have built over a lifetime can affect your ability to diet, as well as the way you feel about failure or success. If you've spent your life telling yourself you are fat and ugly, unlovable unless you are dieting, then you are in a food-and-diet-addictive cycle—a cycle that is incredibly difficult to break.

Such repetition, whether negative or positive, is a great way to learn something. Think about when you learned to drive. At first, you had to think about everything you were doing in a very conscious way. Don't forget to look in the mirror. Don't forget to signal. Is my foot on the gas or the brake? Which pedal is the brake? Oops, not that one! All this information is stored, or encoded, initially in the striatum, in the emotional part of your brain.

As you practice and learn these skills, the information shifts to another part of the striatum. Now they've become habits, automatic—you no longer have to consider these actions consciously; you just do them, unconsciously. Emotions work in the same way, only it is feelings and memories that get stored in your brain.

We have to recognize that our lifelong habits are hardwired in our brain circuits—our neurological pathways—and that changing them is the key to changing ourselves.

KEY NOTE:
You *can* teach an old dog new tricks!

Just as you can learn to drive, or play tennis or speak another language, you can learn not to yell at someone or reach for that drink. Using the principles of *neuroplasticity*—the brain's ability to reorganize and change by forming new synapses, or neural connections—you can retrain your brain.

Managing those MiGGi moments

The distinction between how the brain reacts and how it responds is an important one. Acting out of instinct motivated by MiGGi, the emotional part of the brain reacts in milliseconds, unconsciously. It takes a few seconds for Thinker, the rational part of your brain, to stop and consider how to respond in a healthy, positive way.

Unlike the cats in the cucumber videos, we can recognize our MiGGi moments and learn to pause or stop them at will. Whenever I am having a MiGGi moment, instead of letting my brain drive my normal reaction, like eating some chocolate, I stop and take a deep breath. This immediately reduces my heart rate. It also reminds me to tell myself that whatever it is, it's a cucumber, not a snake.

Each time I do this, my brain is learning that a racing heart does not mean there's anything to be afraid of. When I let my brain feel the MiGGi moment, stop, take a deep breath, and do something else, I'm teaching it that this is the new normal reaction to stress.

Our brains are a lot stronger than we think, with an almost unlimited capacity for resilience when given the opportunity to unlock from stress or worry. When I started to acknowledge my MiGGi moments, held my breath, and let them go, I felt a remarkable sense of relief. This is how we start to teach the brain to be resilient.

Here's a good way to begin: Smile at someone. When a person smiles back at you, he or she is literally mirroring your action. Put simply, mirror neurons activate and boost positive neurochemicals in your brain—and in the brain of the other person, too.

ANDREA'S STORY: Breathing through stress

Andrea is thirty-nine years old, raising two children under the age of ten. One morning, she had just dropped the kids off at school and was on her way to work when her ex-partner called and asked if he could have the kids for Christmas. Since the children had been with him the previous Christmas, Andrea immediately got angry, and they began to argue. After an hour more of driving, she got to work and was about to head into a meeting with her boss when a member of her team called in sick.

The meeting was an important one, about strategies to increase sales and the new processes the new management was putting in place. Early on, Andrea caught herself staring out the window in a frozen state and realized she was no longer paying attention. In other words, she was having a MiGGi moment. She pushed her shoulders back and took a deep breath. As her heart rate slowed, she began to relax, and for that moment, she let it all go—the argument about Christmas, the missing colleague…. She reminded herself that she was safe, that everything would work out, and was able to return to the conversation.

Take a brain break

Andrea had trained her brain to notice when she was having a MiGGi moment and to respond by taking a brain break: pushing her shoulders back, taking a deep breath, and doing her best to let go of what was bothering her. The deep breathing and letting go deactivated MiGGi and strengthened Thinker.

Brain-imaging studies have demonstrated that the activity in the brain caused by deep breathing, meditation, and mindfulness exercises are all powerful ways of controlling your brain and emotions.[44,45] People who meditate or practice mindfulness report feeling calmer and more focused, too. For some people, though, the thought of sitting crossed-legged and chanting or of trying to meditate for half an hour isn't something they can relate to. Many feel they don't have the time. But **we all have time for deep breathing**.

TRY THIS:
Breathe in through your nose for four seconds, then breathe out through your mouth for four seconds.

Get into Koala mode.

Congratulations! You just put a small stop on a MiGGi moment and gave your brain time to catch up. Now, what did you notice? Did you notice that you felt calmer? Did you also notice how many things you were thinking about?

The brain is like an investigator or a scientist. It loves to solve problems and find solutions. And not all thoughts are stressful, of course. You might have been thinking about what you would like for lunch today. Then again, you might have been asking yourself how you were going to pay the mortgage this month.

Either way, take another brain break. Inhale through your nose for four seconds and then, as you exhale through your mouth for four seconds, let go of that thought. You may notice that once you've let go of one thought, another comes flying up to take its place. That's why frequent brain breaks are important.

Don't worry about MiGGi moments at first. To get started, try simply breathing in for four counts and then out for four counts. Do this several times a day: when you wake up in the morning, before you go to sleep, when you are stuck in traffic, standing in a line, or have a free moment at work. Once you get used to doing this and only this, it will be easier to start deeply breathing in and out when a negative thought arises.

EMMA'S STORY: Responding to MiGGi moments meant finally getting some sleep

Night after night, Emma, a woman in her mid-forties, would wake up and not be able to go back to sleep. She had many reasons to worry about her kids, and night after night, she lay awake thinking about one of them and one or more of their problems, not that she ever came up with a solution or resolved anything. Not getting a good night's sleep left her feeling more stressed and worried, of course, but she just could not break the cycle.

The brain is a learning machine, and when Emma went over her worries about the future, she was teaching her brain to do that every time she woke up. Finally, she tried something different. Each time she woke up, she did some deep breathing. She was surprised at how soon she started sleeping again.

By putting a pause on MiGGi—allowing her brain to stop for a second, rather than rushing into the next worry or thought—she broke the cycle. Doing the deep-breathing exercises over and over again, she taught her brain a new response to stress. Learning to calm MiGGi down gave Thinker time to engage and make a more rational response to the stressful situation.

> **KEY NOTE:**
> A daily brain break is a way to train the brain to pause **MiGGi** and give Thinker time to respond.

Calm your brain through tracing

Occasionally, I feel so stressed out that taking deep breaths and letting go does not work. That's when *doing* something is best. This is my favorite way of stopping those MiGGi moments. Take a fine-point pen and spend at least five minutes tracing the lines in the picture. Work as slowly and precisely as you can. If you still feel stressed while you are tracing, take a deep breath in and let it out. Write down what is bothering you, and then practice letting it go. Tracing slowly and precisely is a great way to focus your brain on one task, and this strengthens Thinker and calms MiGGi.[46-48] Try this every day for as little or as long as you like. More tracing pages are provided at the end of the book.

Write here anything that you noticed while tracing.
Then take a deep breath, exhale, and let it go.

_____

_____

_____

_____

_____

_____

_____

_____

_____

_____

_____

_____

_____

_____

_____

_____

_____

_____

Tracing slowly and precisely

ANABEL'S STORY, continued: Healthier MiGGi moments

Remember Anabel, whose sugar addiction began as an infant? Once she realized that she'd never lose weight and keep it off unless she reduced her sugar intake, she started paying attention to when she craved sugar most. She found her strongest cravings came after a bad day at work, and the biggest culprit was ice cream, which she'd consume between seven and ten p.m. For the next thirty days, she went for a walk or did the tracing exercise instead. After a month, these actions became more habitual, and it became easier to head out the door or pull out the tracing paper.

Stress is not always bad for the brain. Stress can motivate us to reach deadlines, perform well during a sports or other competition, work hard to achieve a goal.

STACY'S STORY: Dealing with good and bad stress

Stacy, forty-five, is a reporter on a daily newspaper. She's long recognized that having an imminent deadline—and "I always have a pending deadline"—is stressful. The good news is, she always made her deadlines. The bad news is, she usually coped by eating a bag of cookies while she was writing. After getting the story to her editor, she would relax with a martini, although "I had no idea that constant stress from looming deadlines was connected to sipping martinis."

Now that she is aware when she's having a MiGGi moment, she no longer reacts impulsively. "I say to myself, 'C'mon, it is just a MiGGi moment. Stop and go outside for a minute, look up and breathe.

The deadline is not going to kill me. I am safe." The more she did this, the clearer it became that her MiGGi moments were driving much of her eating and drinking. "Now I'm able to stop them, to give me just enough time to engage Thinker and make a more reasoned response, like going outside."

However much we work at calming MiGGi, stressful situations still arise and old patterns still emerge. If you find that you're not remembering to take deep breaths, or are forgetting to let the stressful thoughts go when you exhale, take action. It might be easier to remember to do something, like Stacy does: go outside, get a glass of water, touch your toes, swing your arms, walk around the room.

ROSE'S STORY: Moving through stress

In her forties, Rose decided she wanted to change her career and went back to school. Here's how she describes one MiGGi moment and how she dealt with it. "I had a homework assignment that I knew was going to be difficult, so I was a bit nervous sitting down to start it. As soon as I began reading phrases such as 'fundamental knowledge' and 'qualitative discontinuities,' I felt worse. I recognized I was having a MiGGi moment, though, and instead of finding a million reasons to stop working on the assignment, I did something else."

Rose had learned to deal with her MiGGi moments by breathing deeply, touching her toes, and doing some knee lifts. "Then I returned to my desk and worked for two hours straight. Wow. Stopping and exercising for a few minutes gave me time to stop thinking about all the reasons I would not be able to complete the work, and all the reasons for doing the assignment now. I made a more rational response and overcame my procrastination, something I have had to deal with most of my life."

> ## KEY NOTE:
> Doing something like deep breathing, tracing, or moving your body on a daily basis paves the way for your brain to establish new habits — to replace the old reactions with reasoned responses — and also begins to trim the body.

Identify one sugar- or fat-filled food that you use to relieve stress

That's the easy part. Now, for the next week, instead of reaching for those chips or that chocolate, take a brain break, do the tracing exercise, stand instead of sit, go for a walk, touch your toes, or, if you're really hungry, have a healthier snack. Remember, **the brain does not care where you get the feel-good chemicals to relieve stress**.

KEY NOTE:
Balance stress with healthy rewards.
The brain does not care where you
get the feel-good chemicals.

Training the brain to stop MiGGi and give Thinker center stage may sound like a superpower, and in a way it is. You won't fly faster than a speeding bullet, but you'll be able to tackle an unconscious response to stress by doing something about it. In fact, just standing like a superhero can stop a MiGGi moment in its tracks.

POWER POSE: The high-power position

Taking a stance like Wonder Woman or Superman for just two minutes can reduce the stress hormone, cortisol, and increase the power hormone, testosterone. In a TED Talk[49], Dr. Amy Cuddy, describes research that has shown that the high-power posture is a great brain hack, a fine way of tapping into the natural biochemistry in our brains and bodies to calm MiGGi and feel more confident.[50] You don't want to be in the low-power position: closed in, with your shoulders slumped. For the next two minutes, take the high-power position — stand up and push your shoulders back — and see how that makes you feel. You will immediately notice a difference.

This is a great way to start the day. Practice in front of the mirror every morning, maybe after you brush your teeth, and several times throughout the day. That alone will help reduce the impact of MiGGi moments. Later, instead of heading to the vending machine if you're nervous about a meeting or have a tight deadline, head into the bathroom and take the power pose.

A day in the life of achieving your body and life goals

When we take daily steps or actions toward attaining our goals, instead of blaming past events or other people for our inability to achieve them, we are keeping the brain centered and moving forward. It calms MiGGi and keeps Thinker clear and in command. When MiGGi is calm, the brain has time to control its impulses, make better short-term decisions, and plan for the future. This gives us a greater capacity to execute and achieve long-term goals.[51]

Working on plans over which we have some control and following through, rather than worrying about something we can't change, is really healthy for the brain.[51] It is an excellent way to reduce stress. Plus: We get something accomplished!

Write down one thing you'd like to achieve, then create simple daily steps you can take toward attaining that goal. For example, your goal is getting more exercise. Before you even get out of bed, breathe in for four seconds and out for four seconds. Then, as soon as you get up, put on your walking or running shoes. Even if you only walk to the mailbox or around your house or apartment, you'll get some exercise, and pretty soon you'll feel like doing more.

If your goal is to eat less junk food, choose one high-fat or sugary food you eat when you are stressed. Then notice when you feel stressed or are having a MiGGi moment, and instead of going to the vending machine or the fridge, do something else, like going for a walk or taking the power pose.

Or maybe you want to write a book. You've been thinking about it for five years. Yes, it's a daunting task, so break it down into smaller tasks. Each day, write one sentence, good or bad; then write two sentences each day. Within a month, you will have written some fifteen pages. Keep going. Instead of waiting another five years, until after the kids have left school or whatever you've told yourself, you will have written that book.

Set simple goals: walking or doing exercises for ten minutes or having one less sugar-sweetened drink every day for the next seven days. Don't think about it; just do it! Don't give your brain a chance to come up with any excuses or other plans: It's too cold or too hot now; I'll do it after work, or I'll do it after I leave the kids at school, or I will wait until after the party on the weekend. It is the small daily steps that train the brain to generate long-term healthy habits.

It is better to do something small every day than to do one workout a week or eat well one day a week. Training the brain using the principles of neuroplasticity requires repetitive daily practice. Before long, you will have trained your brain to manage stress and make better choices around food and exercise. **The easiest way to get started is to get started.**

Then write a list of goals you want to achieve in the next five days, and then in the next month. Choose *one* goal, break it down into steps you can take toward achieving it, and list the things you need to do to make that goal a reality.

Taking daily steps and actions keeps the brain present and looking forward. As we reach our goals and execute our dreams, we start to realize our purpose—and there is nothing more powerful and healthy for the brain and the body than knowing that we are living our purpose.[52]

Write down one goal you have
to manage stress or trim your body

Examples: To become more aware of MiGGi moments,
exercise more, eat less sugar or drink less alcohol,
not struggle with my weight

Write goal here: _____

Write down the obstacles that have
stopped you so far

Examples: I don't have enough time to exercise, I don't pay attention
to what I eat or drink, I look after everyone else

_____

_____

Five days and daily steps to begin
to train the brain to move the body

Goal: **To move your body more**

Step 1: Figure out how much you are moving your body
every day.

Step 2: As soon as you get out of bed, go for a walk.

Step 3: Move your body more: standing instead of sitting,
walking, exercising, taking the stairs. Record the number
of minutes and what you did below.

Day 1. _____

Day 2. _____

Day 3. _____

Day 4. _____

Day 5. _____

Write down one goal you've wanted to achieve for a long time

Examples: To change my career or job, get a promotion, improve my relationship with my partner or child, study, write a book, save for retirement, learn a language

Write goal here: _____

Write down the obstacles that have stopped you so far

Examples: Fear of failure or change, have not studied for a long time, feel too comfortable in my job, not enough money, not good enough, the kids, too many debts, have to pay for college or my retirement, too old, cannot be bothered

_____

_____

Five days and daily steps to begin to train the
brain to move forward toward that goal

Goal: **To get a new job or career**

Step 1: Think about what you love to do at work. Why do you want to change?

Step 2: Work out what experience, study, or personal development is needed to get a new job or career.

Step 3: What will you be proud to have achieved in your work?

Step 4: Write below what you did to move forward. Examples: Set a deadline to make the change, updated resume, worked out why you are unhappy with what you are doing, explored the study requirements, looked for job opportunities, asked people why they are happy in their work or career.

Step 5: Repeat step four for the next five days or until you have achieved your goal.

Day 1. _____

Day 2. _____

Day 3. _____

Day 4. _____

Day 5. _____

KEY NOTE:
There is nothing more powerful and healthy for the brain and body than knowing that we are living our purpose.

PRINCIPLE 4:

Manage stress by eating and drinking fewer sugar-containing and high-fat foods and beverages

Reducing sugar, fat, and alcohol intake; managing stress with healthy rewards

PRINCIPLE 4: Manage stress by eating and drinking fewer sugar-containing and high-fat foods and beverages

When we're not feeling healthy and good about our bodies, it's harder to go out into the world with confidence and purpose. But to get healthy and trim, we have to be aware of how our brain is dictating what we are eating, how much we are eating, and how much or how little we are exercising.

SELENA'S STORY: Eating more and more without knowing it

In the past, in response to a stressful day in the lab, I would have (in no particular order) candies and chocolates, a glass or two of wine, and a second serving of my favorite foods at dinner. This was my brain's particular reaction to stress.

The impulse to treat stress with sugar went all the way back to my youth. I grew up in a small town in Australia in which there wasn't a lot to do. When I was a teenager, we would hang out at the local swimming pool with a bag of assorted candies, carefully selected from among the pineapples, sherbet cones, and what we called false teeth. Even then, there was something special about these afternoons, and they formed an indelible memory. My brain learned to equate happiness with eating sweets.

It didn't take long for my brain to take the extra step and recognize that eating sweets relieved stress. That became my autopilot stress response.

I can still remember how large the appetizers and entrees appeared to me when I first moved to the United States. After awhile, of course, the size of the portions looked normal, and whenever I went back to Australia, I wondered what had happened to the food, the servings looked so small.

Having an unconscious sense of how much I'd need on my plate to feel satisfied made it even harder to control my eating. The amount of food I consumed at each meal increased so slowly that I wasn't aware of it.

I recall so clearly when a colleague who was never afraid to say what he thought commented on how much I could eat. I thought, A grilled chicken *panini* with provolone is a fairly normal-size lunch; what is he talking about? Now I see that I was consuming six hundred and fifty calories at that one meal—then returning to my desk and sitting for another four or five hours. And as we get older, the amount of energy we need from our food declines, so we don't burn up those calories as quickly as we did when we were young.

It's disturbing to think how unaware I was of how much food I was eating and how much weight I was gaining. Since my attention was on everything else, I didn't see what was happening right in front of me.

And, looking back, I see that I never felt full, even after eating a whole bowl of pasta and meat sauce and a big salad and drinking a glass of wine. **The more I ate, the more I wanted to eat**, which is similar to other types of addiction. Remember the feel-good chemicals, such as dopamine, in the striatum? Research has shown that the more we eat/drink/take drugs, the less available the dopamine receptors are. That means that we have to eat more/drink more/take more drugs in order to feel the same level of pleasure.

Sugar is addictive:
The more you have, the more you want

Our research had long focused on alcohol addiction. When we turned our attention to the effects of sugar on the brain, it was initially as a control for our experiments with alcohol—until the day my collaborator, an expert in nicotinic receptors, called me, aghast, and said, "Can you believe this? Sugar is having exactly the same effect on the brain as alcohol and nicotine."

Sugar, we discovered, is as addictive as nicotine, one of the most addictive drugs in the world. We spent the next five years mapping, verifying, and replicating that discovery before confirming it and publishing a series of papers on the topic.[1,2] The shocking finding was that **sugar disrupts the brain pathways in exactly the same way as alcohol and nicotine.** Sugar activates a neurotransmitter that activates the nicotinic receptors, the receptors that nicotine binds to. And by the way, artificial sweeteners are as addictive as sugar.

The toxic effects of added sugars to the diet were discovered by Dr. Robert Lustig.[76,77] Like nicotine and alcohol, sugar disrupts signals to both Thinker and MiGGi. It affects our impulse control—making it harder to resist after the first bite—and our reward center—making us want more and more. **Reduced impulse control and increased pleasure seeking is one of the reasons sugar is so addictive.**[53] If you're someone who stopped smoking, you know that if you had just one cigarette today, even if it's thirty years later, you could easily start smoking again. That's because nicotine leaves an "indelible memory" of a pleasurable experience.[54]

Whether sugar, alcohol, or nicotine, the more you have, the more you want. Craving more sugar and giving in to that urge, of course, leads to further weight gain. And the higher our body mass index (BMI), the more difficult it is to stop.[55,56] Simply put, the heavier we are, the harder it is to stop eating high-fat foods and sugar. Studies conducted with obese adolescents indicate that they had reduced executive function, or impulse control, compared with adolescents of normal weight. Brain-imaging studies showed that these teens had less connectivity between the prefrontal cortex (the impulse-control center) and the reward centers of the brain.[57-60] In other words, MiGGi was overpowering Thinker.

> ## KEY NOTE:
> Eating sugar makes us want to eat
> more sugar. That's one of the reasons
> it is so hard to whittle our muffin tops.

Why sugar makes us eat more, not less

Sucrose, or table sugar, is the basic sugar we all know and love. **Sucrose = fructose + glucose.** That is, sucrose breaks down into fructose and glucose, which have the same number of calories but affect the body in completely different ways.[61]

Glucose, also known as blood sugar, is the key source of energy for our bodies and brains. It's either used immediately or, as glycogen, is stored in muscle cells or the liver for later use. Insulin, an important hormone, regulates blood sugar—for one thing, it **lets the brain know that you're full** and can stop eating. Insulin is secreted when your glucose levels are elevated. Insulin is what facilitates the entry of glucose into your liver and muscle cells.

Fructose is found naturally in many fruits and vegetables—and is now present in up to 75 percent of all foods—but it is not the preferred energy source for muscles or the brain. It **stimulates the feeding center of the brain,** the hypothalamus; it tells your brain that you're not full and to keep eating.[62, 63] Fructose is metabolized only in the liver and is more *lipogenic*, or fat-producing, than glucose.

Fructose and the fat cells

Remember Bethany and that five-hundred-calorie scone she ate on the way home from the gym? It was almost 50 percent fat and 25 percent sugar. She would have been much better off eating a five-hundred-calorie snack that contained less sugar and fat. Why? **Calories consumed in the form of sugar are not the same as calories from other foods.**

What happens to fat cells when we lose and regain weight

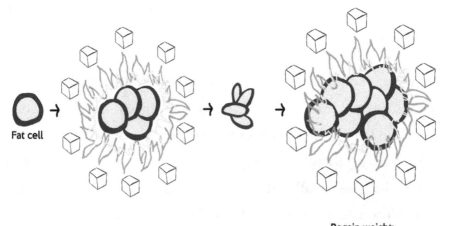

Fat cell

| Starting weight | Gain weight | Lose weight | Regain weight:
Worse off than before
losing weight |

Adapted from Source: bodyconsciousnessblog.com

The average chocolate bar contains about two hundred and thirty calories and is about 50 percent sugar. An avocado with the same number of calories consists of just 0.2 percent sugar. **The fat produced from the sugar in a candy bar is more than fifty times that in an avocado.** You can see how much more work it is to burn off the sugar in the candy bar than in the avocado.

While the calories from glucose are stored in your muscle cells or liver, **the calories from fructose are converted into fat** and stored in the adipose tissue, or fat cells, which lines the stomach, thighs, and butt.[64-66] This is what leads to jelly bodies, jiggly thighs, love handles, and muffin tops.

The body triggers your fat cells to release energy only when it is not getting energy from anywhere else. From a primitive survival perspective, when you don't know where the next meal is coming from, that's important. Most people, at least in wealthier societies, have the opposite problem: the incredible amount of high-calorie and sugary food tempting us in workplaces, stores, and homes every single day.

KEY NOTE:
Fructose makes you fat.

The body actually contains two types of fat. *Visceral fat* gathers at your waistline and *subcutaneous fat* lies under your skin. High levels of fructose increase visceral fat. In addition to expanding your waistline, this type of fat increases your chances of developing chronic diseases such as type-two diabetes, cardiovascular disease, obesity, and metabolic syndrome.[67-69] Even more alarming, when fructose is present in children's fat cells as they mature, their bodies are less able to respond to insulin in both belly fat and skin fat, which is a marker for type-two diabetes[69]—another reason not to fall into the sugar habit as a child.

In addition, **even low levels of chronic exposure to stress hormones stimulate the growth of fat cells.**[70-72] Extended periods of exposure to stress hormones, such as cortisol, caused by such things as too little sleep, lead to bigger fat cells.

KEY NOTE:
Stress grows our fat cells, too.

Fat cells can shrink, but they never disappear. When you "lose" body fat, the fat cell stays right where it was, under the skin and on top of the muscles, which is why you can't see muscle "definition" when your body fat is high. **The key to shrinking your fat cells is not giving them excess energy to store.**

Like fatty foods, cigarettes, and alcohol, sugar can be tough to resist (especially if you're stressed or when someone brings cupcakes to work to celebrate a birthday or promotion). Ask anyone who regularly enjoys that perfectly glazed donut, that creamy chocolate bar, that sweet, fizzy soda, those salty fries, those crispy chips. Even worse, when you try to give them up, you can experience a withdrawal similar to alcohol and nicotine withdrawals.

ANABEL'S STORY, continued: Detoxing from sugar

Anabel began by reducing her sugar intake, specifically by avoiding the ice cream she'd habitually turned to after a stressful day at work. Then she decided to go cold turkey. But quitting all sugar after thirty years wasn't easy. "I went through five weeks of painful withdrawal to get sugar out of my system," she remembers. During the first two weeks, while she felt the cravings weren't too bad, she had headaches and achy bones. By the third week, however, she was becoming emotional over trivial things and found herself unable to think clearly.

These symptoms may sound familiar to anyone who has attempted to break an alcohol habit. Detoxing from sugar is not dissimilar from detoxing from alcohol, but it is easier to wean yourself from it.

To manage the unpleasant process of withdrawal, gradually reduce your sugar intake, especially the sugar that comes from comfort eating, like Anabel's ice cream.

KEY NOTE:
Don't quit eating sugar all at once; slowly reduce the amount you eat.

WATCH OUT: Sugar is everywhere

Fructose has always been present in our diets, but we're consuming more sugar than ever before. The amount of soda or sugar-sweetened beverages that we drink, for instance, has increased fivefold since 1950. But sugar isn't found in only the obvious places, like donuts, cupcakes, and soda. Sugar is embedded in the food chain. Data from the National Health and Nutrition Examination Survey and the U.S. Department of Agriculture has shown that **75 percent of all foods and beverages contain sugar.**[73,74] (There are many resources you can read to understand more about the toxic effects of excess sugar on the brain and body.[75-77])

> You'd be surprised by the amount of sugar in some common foods

Do you know how much sugar you eat every day?

Here's how to find out: Look at the nutrition label on the back of the package or can. Now look at what's written in the carbohydrates section. Remember, the values shown on the label are based on one serving. If the serving size is three cookies and you ate six, you consumed double the amount of sugar listed on the label.

If there is no label, you can use an online nutritional database. The most comprehensive such databases are the USDA Food Composition Databases, at ndb.nal.usda.gov/ndb/.[78]

List five items you ate today and how much sugar is in each one:

1. _____

2. _____

3. _____

4. _____

5. _____

You know how people like to post photos of beautiful dishes or meals on Facebook or Instagram? Start taking a photograph of every single thing you eat and drink in a day. Compile the images into a photo library in a notebook or pad, then note how much sugar each contains. This Wiki website will be of great help: wikihow.com/Count-Your-Sugar-Intake.[79]

This website also talks about **added sugar**, such as when you're drinking coffee or baking cookies. The American Heart Association recommends that women get no more than one hundred calories a day from added sugar; men, no more than a hundred and fifty calories per day.[80] One teaspoon equals four grams of sugar. One gram of sugar has four calories; thus, one teaspoon of added sugar contains sixteen calories. Think about that next time you add sugar to your coffee.

As I think we all know, losing weight calls for taking in fewer calories. My focus is on MiGGi moments, not dieting; but now that I've mentioned calories, here are some quick figures and some helpful advice. Most women can lose weight safely by taking in twelve hundred to fifteen hundred calories a day. Men, women who are more overweight—and women who exercise regularly—can drop pounds safely by eating fifteen hundred to eighteen hundred calories per day. The National Heart, Lung, and Blood Institute's "Aim for a Healthy Weight" website offers information on calorie counts per serving in various foods, from fruits to fats, at healthyeating.nhlbi.nih.gov.[81]

Practice portion control

This illustration conveys recommended portion sizes for some of the foods we eat most often.

Another part of the NIH website looks at "portion distortion." You know those serving sizes I thought were so big when I first came to the United States? They've gotten even bigger.[81]

COMPARISON OF PORTIONS AND CALORIES 20 YEARS AGO AND PRESENT DAY

	20 YEARS AGO		TODAY	
	Portion	Calories	Portion	Calories
Bagel	3" diameter	140	6" diameter	350
Cheeseburger	1	333	1	590
Spaghetti w/meatballs	1 cup sauce 3 small meatballs	500	2 cups sauce 3 large meatballs	1,020
Soda	6.5 ounces	82	20 ounces	250
Blueberry muffin	1.5 ounces	210	5 ounces	500

KEY NOTE:
Be aware of how much you cook, eat, and order in a restaurant.

Now that I can recognize when I'm having a MiGGi moment, I am able to pause, avoid taking "just a small piece of cake" or eating "only one chocolate," and respond more rationally: taking a deep breath, walking, or tracing instead. **The feelings of stress pass quickly and the need to turn to sugar goes away.** I feel full when I eat a normal-size meal and am no longer comforted by high-calorie, sugary food and drink.

I cannot emphasize enough how important reducing my sugar intake was for transforming my brain and my body. It is much easier to strengthen the thinking part of the brain if we calm the emotional part of the brain first.

KEY NOTE:
Without managing stress and reducing sugar and alcohol intake, it is impossible to carve the muffin tops and love handles.

Now it's time to start exercising....

PRINCIPLE 5:

Manage stress through movement

Improving cardio fitness; trimming your body; improving brain plasticity

PRINCIPLE 5:
Manage stress through movement

MUM'S STORY: Exercising keeps her young and fit

Forty years ago, after raising four kids and weathering the many things that life throws at you, my mother was in ill health. At some point, she decided to start walking around the town she lived in. This was very unusual back then; often, she was the only one out in those early-morning hours, walking the streets of her little town. If the weather didn't permit it, she would stride around and around the pool table in her house. My kids love to recall sitting atop the table as Beehar, as they call her, walked circles around them.

My mother now walks for up to two hours every day. If she feels the normal aches and pains, she simply keeps walking. Her parents died from high blood pressure, cancer, and heart disease. My mother has all the susceptibility genes for these disorders, but well into her mid-seventies, she still looks amazing, especially when compared to people of the same age. For her, walking has been the best medicine in the world.

Meanwhile, I kept telling her all the reasons it was impossible for me to find time to exercise. I always felt as if I had ten plates spinning in the air. I did run on a treadmill occasionally, but I never created an exercise routine: If I felt like doing it, I would. If I didn't, I wouldn't. Night after night, I fell asleep on the couch in my work clothes.

My mother called me on my fortieth birthday. At the time, I was living in Berkeley, California, and my parents were in Nanango, a country town in Queensland, Australia. I had just put the kids to bed and was cleaning up the kitchen. "Happy birthday," she said. "Did you have a lovely day?"

"Thanks, Mum. It was a wonderful day. I opened presents in the morning, and the kids made me breakfast in bed. It was great, but now I'm exhausted."

Then Mum said something that caught me off guard. "Well, now that you've turned forty," she commented matter-of-factly, "you have to start exercising."

Our conversation, on my end anyway, instantly went from friendly to heated. "What do you mean 'start exercising'? You know how much I work. Does that mean I have to be up at 3:30 a.m. and 10 p.m. working out?"

"Yes, it does," she replied calmly. While she (or I) may have been exaggerating a little, my mother was absolutely right.

Exercise can make you smarter

Though it didn't take all ten plates to come crashing down, I had to become unhealthy and out of shape before I understood that my mother knew best. You have to exercise every day. Research has shown over and over again that exercise helps keep the body and the brain fit. It decreases the chances of developing chronic diseases such as diabetes, obesity, cardiovascular disease, cancer, dementia, and addiction.[82-86]

Exercise has been shown to reduce stress responses and inflammation.[87] It can increase the expression of genes that promote brain plasticity, including the generation of new neurons and blood vessels.[88] How? By producing BDNF—for brain-derived neurotrophic (growth) factor[89-90]—which supports the production of new synapses, the neural connections in the brain. Increased levels of BDNF stimulate the birth of **new brain cells and new brain pathways.** So **exercise even provides cognitive benefits and increased learning.**

As my mother could tell you, the greatest benefits occur over the long term. At least one study has found a positive association between lifelong physical activity and cognitive function in late middle age.[88] If we really want to train the brain to manage stress and trim the body, physical exercise is by far one of the best ways to get started. Six months of aerobic exercise HAS been shown to modify the way our genes are expressed and increase brain activity.[91-93] Moving our bodies more is a great way to start to train the brain.

> # KEY NOTE:
> ### Exercise makes your brain grow.

It's never too late to start

Think of Charles Eugster, a retired British dentist and "the world's fittest ninety-six-year-old." He took up running, bodybuilding, and rowing when he was eighty, because he was sick of his decrepit old body.[94] He continues to set records; at the age of ninety-five, he broke the British Masters Athletics Federation age-group record for the two-hundred-meter sprint.

In my case, it took not taking care of myself until my body was falling apart, when I was over forty, for my mother's advice to sink in. "You have no choice. You have to exercise." As with anything new, the hardest part was getting started. I had to break a years-long habit of not exercising.

SELENA'S STORY, continued: How I got physical

It may seem extreme, but the goal I set for myself was completing a marathon, or running a twenty-six-mile-long race. I assumed this goal was an impossible one, but it provided the incentive I needed to start running every day. A good friend who is super fit and completes marathons in record times recommended the Napa Valley Trail Marathon, saying it was all downhill, so I signed up.

While the route is gorgeous, weaving through stunning vineyards along the Silverado Trail, it is *not* all downhill. (Never listen to a runner when you plan for your first marathon!) Intimidated but not dissuaded, I downloaded a training schedule and set about preparing to run this marathon. We were living in Brisbane, in Queensland, Australia, at the time, so my training started in a hot and humid place. Every weekend, I ran an extra mile, until I was running twenty-one miles about four weeks before the marathon.

As I increased the number of miles I ran, I noticed I wasn't losing any weight. That seemed strange. Then I read several research articles that showed how sitting for long periods can counteract the effects of aerobic exercise. Even though I was running regularly, I would sit for long periods of time afterward. In terms of weight loss, **all the effort I put into running was being wiped out by sitting all day.**

Once I saw that, I looked into getting a standing desk at work and another for my office at home. In the meantime, I created a tall desk out of packing boxes. The instructions that came with the desk I ordered recommended standing for a short period of time at first. With my stubborn nature, I immediately began standing full-time.

At the end of the first week, I could barely keep my eyes open, I was so exhausted. But already I could see that a number of things had changed. By simply standing all day instead of sitting, I didn't feel cold from the office air conditioning; I felt less hungry; and I could think more clearly. Soon the after-lunch sleepiness went away. Most important, I started to lose weight and saw real progress in my marathon training.

If standing all day is not practical or possible, an adjustable sit-to-stand desk is a good compromise, one the Centers for Disease Control recommends.[95] Standing has benefits similar to walking: It has been shown to increase energy, burn calories, tone muscles, improve posture, and increase blood flow. All this leads to an increase in metabolism and the ability to stay more focused.

KEY NOTE:
Sitting for more than six hours
a day can make us fat and unhealthy.

If standing isn't an option at all, finding another way to move as much as possible is essential. As Charles Eugster says, "If you refer to the Queen of England, who just turned ninety, she has a terrific schedule. She is not somebody who jogs in the park of Buckingham Palace, but she does an enormous amount of standing. She is not someone who sits, and sitting is not healthy."

It has been shown that on average, Americans sit for 7.7 hours a day. Some studies estimate that we sit for up to fifteen hours a day. A study published in the *American Journal of Preventative Medicine* showed that sitting time increased the risk of dying, and this was independent of the level of physical activity.[96]

"For people who sit most of the day," says Martha Grogan, a cardiologist at the Mayo Clinic in Rochester, Minnesota, "the risk of heart attack is about the same as with smoking."

Even worse, according to James A. Levine, Ph.D., an endocrinologist at the Mayo Clinic in Phoenix, Arizona, "Our bodies are breaking down from obesity, high blood pressure, diabetes, cancer, depression, and the cascade of health ills and everyday malaise that come from what scientists have named sitting disease."

As I saw for myself before I began using the standing desk, you cannot reverse "sitting disease" simply by adding more physical activity.[97] My weekly long run was up to nineteen miles, and yet I was lessening the physical benefits by sitting for more than seven hours a day.

KEY NOTE:

You need to do 60 to 75 minutes of exercise every day to counter the effects of sitting for long periods of time. So get up and move!

Shrink those fat cells

As we learned in the previous chapter, sugar and alcohol contribute to the growth of fat cells. These substances give fat cells all the energy they need to keep expanding. To shrink them, we have to reduce their energy sources. Several research studies have shown that exercise is critical to burning the fat stored in those cells.[98,99] We can create an energy deficit—cutting off the energy that fuels the expansion of these cells—by reducing sugar and alcohol intake, practicing portion control, and starting to exercise.

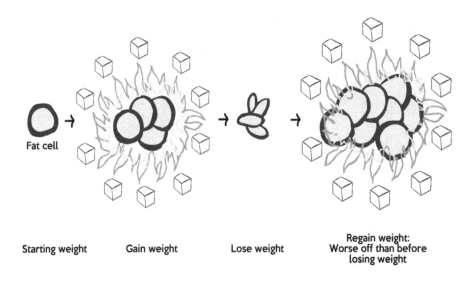

Fat cell

Starting weight   Gain weight   Lose weight   Regain weight: Worse off than before losing weight

It is not possible to get rid of fat cells, but **exercise decreases the size of fat cells and reduces the fat content**. Exciting new research indicates that exercise changes the color of fat cells from white to beige, the color of cells that burn rather than store energy.[98]

There's still debate over whether exercise can help with weight loss. That is, **exercise alone may not help you lose weight.**[100,101] Physical trainers and gym owners worldwide have told me how frustrating it is to see their clients in an endless struggle with their weight despite seeing a change in their bodies. Like Bethany with the post-workout scone, those folks need to think about what they are eating and when.

In any event, exercise is key to trimming the body. A stressful, sedentary lifestyle is one of the leading causes of chronic health problems. Sitting disease is reversible. And exercise is one of the cheapest and easiest ways to modify our genes, strengthen our brains and bodies, and improve our health. The connection is irrefutable and seems obvious. So why is it so hard to get started?

Undo the dopamine stopper

When you sit down to watch TV in the evening, you may plan to watch one show but find that before you know it, two or three hours have gone by. The underlying chemical reaction in your brain is the same as when you intend to eat a handful of potato chips and devour the whole bag. Dopamine, that feel-good chemical in the brain, helps initiate movement as well as motivation. Parkinson's disease, a disorder of the central nervous system that affects movement, is caused by the progressive depletion of dopamine.[102]

To a lesser degree, this is what happens when we sit down for an extended period of time. It gets harder to start moving again. It's the same when we have never exercised: It's so much easier to say, "I can't jog" or "I am too old" or "I hate exercising." These are all automatic responses that we have wired into our brains.

How much are you sitting?

Do you know how much you sit each day? Calculate the number of hours and minutes you spend sitting while eating breakfast, commuting to work, in a meeting, eating lunch, watching TV, at your home computer, eating dinner, reading with the kids. No doubt whatever the total is, it's too much. Find ways to move your body whenever you can.

Calculate how much you sat today,
and write the time in minutes below:

+ At work and in meetings:
+ In the car:
+ Watching television:
+ On a device such as a computer, ipad or phone:
+ Eating:
+ Sleeping:
+ Other:

Some ways to add movement to your day:

+ Move your arms up and down
+ Take the stairs instead of the elevator
+ Get up every hour and get a glass of water
+ Replace sitting with standing as much as you can, e.g., while watching television
+ March around the room
+ Walk wherever possible
+ Play with your kids
+ Take your dog for a walk

SELENA'S STORY, continued: Training the brain in healthy physical habits

Once I started to stand instead of sit and to train for my first marathon, I noticed that I could more easily manage my weight. As exercise became an integral part of my life, I no longer wasted time persuading myself to go for a run; I just put on my running shoes and left. It was so much easier once I had trained my brain to initiate healthy rather than unhealthy habits.

It would be nice to say that within a month of standing all day, I was back to my thirty-year-old body. The pounds that had taken years to gain, however, did not simply fall away. The creep up the scales had stopped. The creep down was a longer journey.

Several sporting events later, I was trimmer. I felt a lot healthier and was proud to be moving my body again, though I was still struggling with that despised muffin top. I moved to strength training to support my core muscles and my back. Strength training supported my running and improved my muscle tone; my metabolism increased, and I slept better. But I had to continue running to keep my weight under control.

What drove the biggest change in my body was cardiovascular training. I'd thought I was fairly fit until I tried running up a hill. I didn't get very far before I was gasping for breath. I've talked with many people who'd also thought they were fit until they began jogging up a flight of stairs or a fairly steep hill.

Several studies have indicated that a certain level of intensity is needed to generate new heart and brain cells. I started small, on a hill near my home, running for ten steps and then walking ten steps. I did this for more than a year. Eventually, I could run uphill for 2.2 miles without stopping. Increasing the intensity of a workout for just five or ten minutes is all it takes to break a sweat.

Much like standing instead of sitting, increasing the intensity of your workout gives you that extra boost. Not only did I feel stronger and more resilient, my muffin top was finally diminishing. Running uphill for fifteen minutes and on a flatter surface for another forty-four minutes each day is what really started to change my body.

But you don't need to run that long to get the added brain and body benefits. Research has shown that **repeated shorts bursts of high-intensity exercise increases levels of BDNF**[89] and other growth factors, and also increases feel-good neurochemicals like **dopamine**

and endorphins. You might start by doing a high-intensity workout — jogging up a flight of stairs or a small incline, say—for ten minutes just three times a week. Then slowly increase the amount of time and the number of days each week.

Exercise is as critical to our lives as drinking water. And going without it can be just as unhealthy. Take it one day at a time and keep going. Stay positive and remember that simple daily steps add up and make a big difference over time.

PRINCIPLE 6:

Love is the antidote to stress

Love is the key to good health, happiness, even survival.

PRINCIPLE 6:
Love is the antidote to stress

Love is the key to good health, happiness, even survival

The first 5 principles in this book focused on stress — on how it wires the brain to create unhealthy habits and how to rewire it. Principle 6 is all about love, in all its forms, because from the day the brain starts developing until the day we take our last breath, love provides the perfect antidote to stress. Love isn't a barrier to stress, but it can keep it from influencing the brain to pursue unhealthy behavior.

After interviewing hundreds of people around the world, I've come to believe that love is something sought by everyone — no matter who you are, where you live, or how much money you have. It's that simple. Why? Our brains are wired that way. Brain imaging has shown that when we think about love, or the feelings associated with love, we activate the limbic system, or what I've called the emotional brain. **Love and attention release pleasure and bonding hormones,** such as endorphins, serotonin, and oxytocin. Love really does make us happier and calmer.

As I described earlier, the three main regions of the brain, which evolved over eons of time, can be considered the survival, emotional, and rational parts. The oldest region is where we record our memories of good and bad experiences, where we feel emotions such as love and fear, anger and joy. It's easy to see how fear—how remembering the dangers of fire or wild animals—can keep you safe. But what's love got to do with it? Everything, especially in the beginning. Think about it: For a newborn baby, a secure bond with a parent or caregiver is perhaps *the* most important survival tool.

Finding love and nourishment are fundamental biological drives. If these basic needs are not met during the first years of life, we will continue to seek love and attention. It's well known that hugs stimulate the release of pleasure and bonding hormones, such as oxytocin and endorphins. These hormones, if released at any time but particularly during the first few years of life, have the capacity to strengthen the brain, to improve executive function and help with learning. This *strengthens the reward circuit* in the brain and *reduces emotional reactivity in the fear center* of the brain.

That's what enables people to cope better with stress as they get older. Studies have shown that unconditional love correlates with fewer adverse childhood experiences, less trauma, and less stress-induced brain wiring. Love and attention from someone, particularly a nurturer or a mentor, provides the foundation for the self-confidence and security that help us overcome many of life's problems.

Conversely, when we can't get these pleasure hormones through love and happiness, we often trigger them in less healthy ways. As we have seen, sugar, caffeine, alcohol, and drugs also activate the brain's reward or feel-good chemicals. If love activates the brain to seek attachment to our parents and then continually seek their approval, parental neglect can lead to behavioral disorders such as addiction and mental health problems. In extreme cases of neglect, studies have found severe deficits in brain activity.

> ## KEY NOTE:
> **Love is a fundamental biological need, providing the foundation for a healthy brain and body.**

"Good genes are nice, but joy is better."

The headline in a 2017 article in the *Harvard Gazette* says it all. The reporter was looking at an ongoing study that began with a look at the physical and mental health of 268 Harvard men, from the classes of 1939-1944, over the course of eighty years and is now researching their offspring. The Harvard Study of Adult Development started in 1938 with what's known as the Grant Study (because a man named W.T. Grant initially funded the research project, at the Harvard University Health Services; the only subjects were men because the university did not yet admit women). In brief, the quality of our relationships was found to be the main "psychosocial predictors of healthy aging."

According to the *Harvard Gazette*, the current research, which includes medical records, in-person interviews, and questionnaires, has found that "close relationships, more than money or fame, are what keep people happy throughout their lives ... Those ties protect people from life's discontents, help to delay mental and physical decline, and are better predictors of long and happy lives than social class, IQ, or even genes."

"The surprising finding is that our relationships and how happy we are in our relationships has a powerful influence on our health," said the study's director, Robert Waldinger, a psychiatrist at Massachusetts General Hospital and professor of psychiatry at Harvard Medical School.

"When the study began, nobody cared about empathy or attachment," added George Vaillant, a psychiatrist who led the study from 1972 to 2004. "But the key to healthy aging is relationships, relationships, relationships."

Another word for that is love.

The idea of love as an antidote to stress may sound like a weak or crazy solution when we're always told to man up, or feel that tough love is the way to go in a tough world. I met a professor of medicine who was incredulous that after so many decades of tracking so many lives, the Harvard study found that the key to a long and happy life is good relationships ... or, as I say, love. He thought the study had gone off track from its original aims and was a failure. This highlights how we so often treat love as a soft and mushy subject, even a throw-away commodity. In fact, **the way the brain processes and stores love is as important as the way it stores any skill**.

> **KEY NOTE:**
> **Love can upend**
> **the genetic lottery.**

Love can be learned

There is nothing like looking great, having a lovely place to live and a nice car to drive. Many of us put most of our efforts into achieving these outward signs of success. All of these things can be purchased, but ultimately none will serve to make us happy in the long run—not if we don't have the love and relationships we need.

We know that love can be passed on in families over the generations. A lack of love can be passed on, too. In Canada, Michael J. Meaney, Ph.D., and his team found that baby rats that were taken from their mothers and never experienced a mother's grooming and licking ("non-handled rats") secreted more stress hormones in response to stress than did the rats that stayed with their mothers and got the normal grooming and licking.

Beyond that, Meaney and other scientists have shown that a mother animal that fails to lick its babies will produce offspring that fail to lick their babies. The cycle repeats over the generations.

But love is an unlimited resource, a free commodity that each of us can tap into. Even if we were not provided love or feel unloved today, **we can teach our brains how to give and receive love.** Like learning to drive or play piano, we can learn to how to hug and kiss and smile and, yes, love.

The easiest way to start is with a smile. Try it and see. Smiling activates the mirror neuron system in the brain of the person you are smiling at. In other words, smiling is a reflex—more often than not, he or she will copy you and smile back. If you smile at yourself in the mirror each morning and throughout the day, and then start smiling at others, it will become a daily practice. This will get the pleasure centers of the brain pumping.

Then you can take the next step. There is no doubt that a bear hug from someone who cares about you can heal a lot of wounds. However, many of us have forgotten how to hug; we're shy about hugging and touching people. But we are all sensory beings, with thousands of nervous connections that need to be stimulated. We all crave to be touched.

Try holding someone's hand. As soon as you do, notice the tension drop in his body, the smile that comes onto her face. You may notice your own feelings of shyness or vulnerability dissipating from the simple motion of putting skin against skin—it is pure magic. You can get pleasure-driving hormones into your brain and body by helping others feel them.

Once you are comfortable holding someone's hand, give that person a hug.

Sometimes hearts get broken

When we give love, our love is not always returned. Love once felt for us sometimes disappears. Elegant brain-imaging studies have shown that **social rejection activates the same parts of the brain as physical pain**. This is why a broken heart hurts so much.

Life has a way of delivering lessons. Before my husband asked me for a divorce, I had a strong opinion when someone seemed to grieve too long over a shattered marriage. "Why doesn't he/she get over it already? It's been years—time to move on!" It wasn't until I was in the same situation that I came to realize that the terrible pain felt by these women and men was absolutely real.

Furthermore, the stress, anger, and pain caused by such rejection can lead us to do things we never imagined possible: pouring expensive wine collections down the drain, engaging private investigators, paying lawyers hundreds of thousands of dollars, spending years in personal and financial battles, running away instead of facing a problem and fixing it. Especially if you are middle-aged, with the security of your family damaged or demolished and your future uncertain, it may feel as if you're entering a bleak, black tunnel with no exit. But you can find that exit if you want to.

JENNIFER'S STORY: How to mend a broken heart

Remember Jennifer, who illustrated Principle 1? That's where I told you about the three parts of the brain, which I call Scout, MiGGi, and Thinker. She had been replaying the events of her heartbreak for more than a decade, yet the details were as vivid as if her husband had just left her. Her brain was keeping her memories alive.

Every time she focused on her divorce, she had a MiGGI moment. I told her that she had "brain lock," and that I could help her unlock it. To do that, she had to start noticing whenever she was having a MiGGi moment, and then to stop and focus on something else: taking a deep breath, going outside, doing some exercises. That's how you begin training the brain to *respond and not react to stress*. Remember, Thinker just needs a few seconds to override MiGGi.

Jennifer learned to start the day by consciously looking out into the beauty of the world; that set her brain in a good direction. When she began paying attention to her MiGGi moments—when she noticed that, once again, she was replaying the story of her divorce—she would take a walk around the block. The story in her brain began fading; her brain became calmer, and she began making better plans for the rest of the day, and beyond.

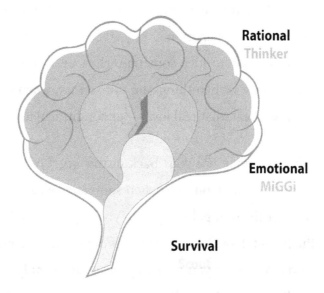

By training her brain to choose a healthier option for her body, she taught it how to stop replaying the memories that kept her so miserable. Before long, she was looking healthier and fitter and slowly taking steps toward change and a better life.

> **KEY NOTE:**
> You can put a shattered heart together again.

Expand the love

When we think about love, it often comes with conditions — it loves the way you look, or your money or career, your family or friends. To be honest, it's easy to love someone when everything is fine and everyone is happy. It's when things are not so rosy, when we don't feel happy or look so great, that real love — unconditional love — steps in.

Knowing that someone has your back in the worst of times can give you the strength to carry on. It is when someone helps you bridge the gap and get over the hump; hugs you in your time of need; holds your hand in the hospital, or during a siege of depression, or grief, or loss — when someone looks you in the eye and says simply, "I am here" — that you discover real love. It is far easier to accept such love when we've learned to love others without conditions.

Often, we act as if there is a quota on love, when it is by far the cheapest thing on the planet. Love not only makes us happy and healthy, it is without bounds. There's no need to fence it in.

The easiest love to give is to our families and direct descendants, who are, after all, extensions of ourselves. The most difficult to give is to people not like ourselves, especially those on the outer rims of social acceptance. When people feel truly loved, however, and secure in this love, they are able to give love to those outside their families and friends, even those they don't know.

You don't have to be Florence Nightingale or Mother Teresa, Nelson Mandela or Martin Luther King, Jr. — people who sometimes put their own lives at risk to help others. A smile, a hug, a positive gesture in word or deed—these are all free and have no quotas.

> ## KEY NOTE:
> ### Love is viral; it radiates outward unless killed by the host.

Seven steps to making love go viral

1. Smiling
2. Holding someone's hand
3. Hugging
4. Kissing
5. Forgiving—yourself and others
6. Giving unconditional love
7. Repeat steps 1 through 6 forever

CONCLUSION

SELENA'S STORY: How I smashed my mindset to love again

I gazed over his shoulder as the moonlight danced and skipped over the water. He wrapped his strong arms around me, and I felt his warm, deep smile fill my body and lift my wings. With that first kiss, my mind was racing. How did this happen? This was not in the plan; I'm not looking for a relationship. At least in this moment of pure joy, all the pain of the past was erased.

He flew into my life as my husband flew out. We met across two different continents and cultures, connected by spirit, linked as if we had known each other for centuries. As fast as love had left, so it returned.

My brain could just as easily have sabotaged this experience by rejecting my feelings, denying me love by fearing the pain and rejection that love had once caused. In fact, many people told me, "Be careful. You've just had your heart broken. Remember what you've been through." But I had developed the tools to love again. As with the parts of my life that I'd already improved by smashing the old, unhealthy mindset — finding better ways to deal with stress, eating healthier food, developing exercise habits that trimmed my body and clarified my thinking — I knew that a broken heart can be stitched back together if you don't dwell on your heartbreak or live in the past. I understood that love really is more important than hate or fear.

That was the key to rebooting my brain, letting in new possibilities and opportunities, and living a more meaningful life. That's what enabled me to love and trust again.

Stress has a way of leaving its imprint on our brains and bodies. We know that, in a learned, habitual, unthinking reaction to stress, it is the emotional part of the brain—what I've called MiGGi—that's encouraging us to eat all those cookies or the rest of the bag of chips, or drink or smoke or do whatever we've found makes us feel better, at least in the short term. MiGGi locks us into unhelpful memories and feelings, too, such as the pain of betrayal or divorce. The brain is a wonderful thing, though. By applying the principles of neuroplasticity, **we can change the way our brains work**.

We can weaken MiGGi and empower Thinker, or the rational part of the brain. This, in turn, can drive dramatic changes to the body. That, in brief, is why MiGGi matters. It starts by recognizing your particular MiGGi moments—what causes you stress and what you habitually do to relieve it—and then learning to pause long enough for the conscious, rational part of your brain to make a different choice, such as taking deep breaths or going for a walk.

When I realized how MiGGi moments were ruling my life and decided to do something about it, it changed everything for me. That's not to say it was easy. It took years to leave my state of denial—to recognize that I was stressed, eating poorly, and not exercising enough, and why. The first eight weeks were the hardest by far. I was working extremely hard at cutting back on sugar and alcohol and exercising more, and I could not see any results. I started thinking, What is the point? It's been two months and I look exactly the same! I wish I'd noticed more quickly that I felt better able to manage stress. That was the key.

Stress is all around us, and much if not most of it is beyond our control. But managing our stress is completely within our control. Stress and its impact on the wiring of the brain is a prime reason that diet and exercise programs are rarely successful in the long term. (When they are, it's because the person stayed with the program long enough for a change in lifestyle.) As soon as the next major stressful event occurs, we tend to fall back into the unhealthy eating and drinking habits that caused us to gain weight in the first place. Stress goes straight back into our bodies.

So we need to understand the impact of stress on the brain and what to do about it. **One thing is certain: We cannot change the past. We can change the brain.** Indeed, the beautiful thing about the brain is its enormous capacity for change, its ability to heal, and its untapped potential. I would love to see the term *mental health* replaced with the term *brain health*. I would love to see people discussing the brain and retraining it in the same way they talk about their bicep and quad workouts at the gym.

The hardest part is staying with the daily practice long enough so that it feels less of a struggle and begins to become your new lifestyle. Remember, if this were easy, everyone would be fit, trim, happy, and loving, and the world would be a peaceful place. We can start by drawing a line in the sand, crossing over it, and not looking back. Smashing mindset starts by keeping the brain focused on the present and moving forward, managing stress and developing lifelong healthier habits, one step at a time.

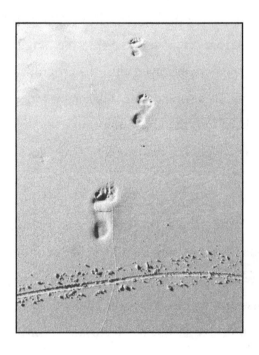

EXERCISES

Develop one healthy habit to manage stress and trim the body

Pausing MiGGi and giving Thinker time to make a healthier choice

It is difficult to trim the body in the long term without being aware of how your stress reactions drive what you eat and drink and how much you move your body. We have to teach the brain to pause MiGGi moments to give Thinker time to turn stress reactions from an unhealthy to a healthy response. **Choose one unhealthy habit to work on first.**

For example, after a hard day at work, you may have a glass of wine or beer or eat a bag of chips to relieve the stress. Instead of going into the kitchen when you get home, each day for the next four weeks do something else, like going for a walk, tracing, taking a deep breath, or exercising for five minutes. Learning to manage and then change stress reactions is the first step. It takes repetitive daily practice and actions.

For the next four weeks, record your MiGGi moments, what triggered the stress, the food and beverages you chose to relieve the stress, how often you moved your body, and the healthy response you made instead. There are tracing pages and a place to take notes provided for each week.

MiGGi MOMENTS TRACKER

Week One

WEEK 1: Notice and Pause MiGGi to Manage Stress and Trim the Body

Choose one habit to work on

Date Daily steps	Number of MiGGi moments	MiGGi triggers	Unhealthy habit: Food, drink, exercise choices	Healthy habit: What I did to pause MiGGi and the healthy choice I made instead

TRACING PAGES FOR WEEK ONE

Trace as slowly and precisely as possible

Trace as slowly and precisely as possible

Trace as slowly and precisely as possible

WEEK 1: Notes

WEEK 1: Notes

WEEK 1: Notes

WEEK 1: Notes

WEEK 1: Notes

WEEK 1: Notes

MiGGi MOMENTS TRACKER

Week Two

WEEK 2: Notice and Pause MiGGi to Manage Stress and Trim the Body

Choose one habit to work on

Date Daily steps	Number of MiGGi moments	MiGGi triggers	Unhealthy habit: Food, drink, exercise choices	Healthy habit: What I did to pause MiGGi and the healthy choice I made instead

TRACING PAGES FOR WEEK TWO

Trace as slowly and precisely as possible

Trace as slowly and precisely as possible

Trace as slowly and precisely as possible

WEEK 2: Notes

WEEK 2: Notes

WEEK 2: Notes

WEEK 2: Notes

WEEK 2: Notes

WEEK 2: Notes

MiGGi MOMENTS TRACKER

Week Three

WEEK 3: Notice and Pause MiGGi to Manage Stress and Trim the Body

Choose one habit to work on

Date Daily steps	Number of MiGGi moments	MiGGi triggers	Unhealthy habit: Food, drink, exercise choices	Healthy habit: What I did to pause MiGGi and the healthy choice I made instead

TRACING PAGES FOR WEEK THREE

Trace as slowly and precisely as possible

Trace as slowly and precisely as possible

Trace as slowly and precisely as possible

WEEK 3: Notes

WEEK 3: Notes

WEEK 3: Notes

WEEK 3: Notes

WEEK 3: Notes

WEEK 3: Notes

MiGGi MOMENTS TRACKER

Week Four

WEEK 4: Notice and Pause MiGGi to Manage Stress and Trim the Body

Choose one habit to work on

Date Daily steps	Number of MiGGi moments	MiGGi triggers	Unhealthy habit: Food, drink, exercise choices	Healthy habit: What I did to pause MiGGi and the healthy choice I made instead

TRACING PAGES FOR WEEK FOUR

Trace as slowly and precisely as possible

Trace as slowly and precisely as possible

Trace as slowly and precisely as possible

WEEK 4: Notes

WEEK 4: Notes

WEEK 4: Notes

WEEK 4: Notes

SOURCE NOTES

1. Neuronal nicotinic acetylcholine receptor modulators reduce sugar intake.
Shariff M, Quik M, Holgate J, Morgan M, Patkar OL, Tam V, Belmer A, Bartlett SE.
PLoS One. 2016 Mar 30; 11(3).

2. Prolonged consumption of sucrose in a binge-like manner, alters the morphology of medium
spiny neurons in the nucleus accumbens shell.Klenowski PM, Shariff MR, Belmer A, Fogarty
MJ, Mu EW, Bellingham MC, Bartlett SE. Front Behav Neurosci. 2016 Mar 23; 10:54.

3. The antihypertensive drug pindolol attenuates long-term but not short-term binge-like
ethanol consumption in mice. Patkar OL, Belmer A, Holgate JY, Tarren JR, Shariff MR, Morgan
M, Fogarty MJ, Bellingham MC, Bartlett SE, Klenowski PM. Addict Biol. 2016 Jan 11.

4. Varenicline, an alpha4beta2 nicotinic acetylcholine receptor partial agonist, selectively
decreases ethanol consumption and seeking.Steensland P, Simms JA, Holgate J, Richards JK,
Bartlett SE. Proc Natl Acad Sci U S A. 2007 Jul 24; 104(30): 12518-23.

5. Early Life Stress, Nicotinic Acetylcholine Receptors and Alcohol Use Disorders.
Holgate JY, Bartlett SE. Brain Sci. 2015 Jun 30; 5(3): 258-74.

6. Emotion circuits in the brain. LeDoux JE. Annu Rev Neurosci. 2000; 23: 155-84.

7. The BRAIN Initiative: developing technology to catalyse neuroscience discovery.
Jorgenson LA, et al. Philos Trans R Soc Lond B Biol Sci. 2015 May 19; 370(1668).

8. Soft-Wired: How the New Science of Brain Plasticity Can Change Your Life. Merzenich M. M.
(2013). San Francisco: Parnassus Publishing. see http://www.brainhq.com/

9. Brain plasticity-based therapeutics. Merzenich MM, Van Vleet TM, Nahum M. Front Hum
Neurosci. 2014 Jun 27; 8: 385

10. Perceptual learning and adult cortical plasticity.
Gilbert CD, Li W, Piech V. J Physiol. 2009 Jun 15; 587(Pt 12): 2743-51.

11. Rule learning enhances structural plasticity of long-range axons in frontal cortex.
Johnson CM, Peckler H, Tai LH, Wilbrecht L. Nat Commun. 2016 7: 10785.

12. The striatum: where skills and habits meet. Cold Spring Harb Perspect Biol. 2015 Aug 3;7(8).
Graybiel AM, Grafton ST. Neuron. 2013 Jul 10; 79(1): 16-29.

13. The brain on stress: vulnerability and plasticity of the prefrontal cortex over the life course.
McEwen BS, Morrison JH. Physiol Behav. 2015 Jul 1; 146: 47-56.

14. In pursuit of resilience: stress, epigenetics, and brain plasticity.
McEwen BS. Ann N Y Acad Sci. 2016 Jun; 1373(1): 56-64.

15. Stress-induced structural plasticity of medial amygdala stellate neurons and rapid prevention by a candidate antidepressant. Mol Psychiatry. 2016 May 31. doi: 10.1038/mp. 2016.68. Lau T, Bigio B, Zelli D, McEwen BS, Nasca C.

16. Why diets make us fat: The unintended consequences of our obsession with weight loss. Aamodt, S. http://www.sandraaaamodt.com/.

17. A brief history of the brain. New Scientist tracks the evolution of our brain from its origin in ancient seas to its dramatic expansion in one ape – and asks why it is now shrinking. David Robson. See https://www.newscientist.com/article/mg21128311-800-a-brief-history-of-the-brain.

18. Midbrain circuits for defensive behaviour. Tovote P, Esposito MS, et al. Nature. 2016 Jun 1; 534 (7606): 206-12.

19. Neural control of breathing and CO2 homeostasis. Guyenet PG and Bayliss DA. Neuron. 2015 Sep 2; 87 (5): 946-61.

20. Stress and fear responses in the teleost pallium. Silva PI et al. J Morphol. 1982 Sep; 173 (3): 325-49.

21. Learning about the stress response in this paper and at this website. Recognizing resilience: learning from the effects of stress on the brain. McEwen BS, Gray J, Nasca C. Neurobiol Stress. 2015 Jan 1; 1: 1-11.
see http://www.health.harvard.edu/staying-healthy/understanding-the-stress-response.

22. Acute stress impairs self-control in goal-directed choice by altering multiple functional connections within the brain's decision circuits. Maier SU, Makwana AB, Hare TA. Neuron. 2015 Aug 5;87(3):621-31.

23. Stress and opioids: role of opioids in modulating stress-related behavior and effect of stress on morphine conditioned place preference. Bali A, Randhawa PK, Jaggi AS. Neurosci Biobehav Rev. 2015 Apr; 51: 138-50.

24. The effects of stress exposure on prefrontal cortex: translating basic research into successful treatments for post-traumatic stress disorder. Arnsten AF, Raskind MA, Taylor FB, Connor DF. Neurobiol Stress. 2015 Jan 1; 1: 89-99.

25. Simultaneous changes in sleep, qEEG, physiology, behaviour and neurochemistry in rats exposed to repeated social defeat stress. Ahnaou A and Drinkenburg WH. Neuropsychobiology. 2016; 73 (4): 209-23.

26. Separate circuitries encode the hedonic and nutritional values of sugar. Tellez et al. Nat Neurosci. 2016 Mar; 19 (3): 465-70.

27. Dietary fat ingestion activates β-endorphin neurons in the hypothalamus. Matsumura et al. FEBS Lett. 2012 Apr 24; 586 (8): 1231-5.

28. Effects of acute ethanol on opioid peptide release in the central amygdala: an in vivo microdialysis study. Lam MP, Marinelli PW, Bai L, Gianoulakis C. Psychopharmacology (Berl) 2008 Dec; 201 (2): 261-71.

29. Cigarette use and striatal dopamine D2/3 receptors: possible role in the link between smoking and nicotine dependence. Okita K, Mandelkern MA, London ED. Int J Neuropsychopharmacol. 2016 Sep 21. pii: pyw074. doi: 10.1093/ijnp/pyw074.

30. Exercise, physical activity, and sedentary behavior in the treatment of depression: broadening the scientific perspectives and clinical opportunities. Hallgren et al. Front Psychiatry. 2016 Mar 11; 7: 36.

31. Dopaminergic neurotransmission in the nucleus accumbens modulates social play behavior in rats. Manduca et al. Neuropsychopharmacology. 2016 Aug; 41(9): 2215-23.

32. Reward, motivation, and emotion systems associated with early-stage intense romantic love. Aron et al. J.Neurophysiol 2005 Jul; 94 (1): 327-37.

33. Nature experience reduces rumination and subgenual prefrontal cortex activation. Bratman GN et al. Proc Natl Acad Sci U S A. 2015 Jul 14; 112 (28): 8567-72.

34. The impacts of nature experience on human cognitive function and mental health. Bratman GN, Hamilton JP, Daily GC. Ann N Y Acad Sci. 2012 Feb; 1249: 118-36.

35. Investing in the future: stimulation of the medial prefrontal cortex reduces discounting of delayed rewards. Cho SS et al. Neuropsychopharmacology 2015 Feb; 40(3): 546-53.

36. Cats vs Cucumbers video link: https://youtu.be/8HGoKN1kjk0

37. Genetic basis of human brain evolution. Vallender EJ1, Mekel-Bobrov N, Lahn BT Trends Neurosci. 2008 Dec; 31 (12): 637-44.

38. Early adverse experiences and the developing brain. Bick J and Nelson CA. Neuropsychopharmacology. 2016 Jan; 41 (1): 177-96.

39. The neuro-environmental loop of plasiticity:a cross-species analysis of parental effects on emotion circuitry development following typical and adverse caregiving. Callaghan BL, Tottenham N. Neuropsychopharmacology. 2016 Jan; 41 (1): 163-76.

40. The long-term impact of adverse caregiving environments on epigenetic modifications and telomeres. Blaze J, Asok A, Roth TL. Front Behav Neurosci. 2015 Apr 8; 9: 79.

41. You can calculate your ACE score here and get access to the papers on Adverse Childhood Experiences (ACE) Study (www.acestudy.org).

42. Childhood adversity and adult chronic disease: an update from ten states and the District of Columbia, 2010. Gilbert LK. Et al. Am J Prev Med. 2015 Mar; 48 (3): 345-9.

43. Adverse childhood experiences and later life adult obesity and smoking in the United States. Rehkopf et al. Ann Epidemiol. 2016 Jul; 26 (7): 488-492. e5.

44. Change in brainstem gray matter concentration following a mindfulness-based intervention is correlated with improvement in psychological well-being. Singelton O et al. Front Hum Neurosci. 2014 Feb 18; 8: 33.

45. 8-week Mindfulness Based Stress Reduction induces brain changes similar to traditional long-termmeditation practice - A systematic review. Gotink RA et al. Brain Cogn. 2016 Oct; 108: 32-41.

46. Functional anatomy of writing with the dominant hand. Horovitz SG et al. PLoS One. 2013 Jul 2; 8 (7): e67931.

47. Drawing and writing: An ALE meta-analysis of sensorimotor activations. Yuan Y and Brown S. Brain Cogn. 2015 Aug; 98: 15-26.

48. Changes in brain activity during motor learning measured with PET: effects of hand of performance and practice. Van Mier H. et al. J Neurophysiol. 1998 Oct; 80 (4): 2177-99.

49. Amy Cuddy's TED talk on the powerpose https://www.ted.com/talks/amy_cuddy_your_body_language_shapes_who_you_are?language=en

50. Leadership is associated with lower levels of stress. Sherman GD et al. Proc Natl Acad Sci U S A. 2012 Oct 30; 109 (44): 17903-7. https://www.ncbi.nlm.nih.gov/pubmed/ 27672175

51. Grit and the brain: spontaneous activity of the dorsomedial prefrontal cortex mediates the relationship between the trait grit and academic performance. Wang S et al. Soc Cogn Affect Neurosci. 2016 Sep 26. pii: nsw 145. [Epub ahead of print]

52. Purpose in life and cerebral infarcts in community-dwelling older people. Yu L et al. Stroke 2015 Apr; 46 (4): 1071-6.

53. Impaired fear extinction retention and increased anxiety-like behaviours induced by limited daily access to a high-fat/high-sugar diet in male rats: Implications for diet-induced prefrontal cortexdysregulation. Baker KD, Reichelt AC. Neurobiol Learn Mem. 2016 Oct 5; 136: 127-138.

54. Nicotine self-administration acutely activates brain reward systems and induces a long-lasting increase in reward sensitivity. Kenny PJ and Markou A. Neuropsychopharmacology. 2006 Jun; 31 (6): 1203-11.

55. Crave, Like, Eat: determinants of food intake in a sample of children and adolescents with a wide range in body mass. Hoffman J et al. Front Psychol. 2016 Sep 21; 7: 1389.

56. Food craving as a mediator between addictive-like eating and problematic eating outcomes. Joyner MA, Gearhardt AN, White MA. Eat Behav. 2015 Dec; 19:98-101.

57. Higher adolescent body mass index is associated with lower regional gray and white matter volumes and lower levels of positive emotionality. Kennedy JT, Collins PF, Luciana M. Front Neurosci. 2016 Sep 8; 10:413.

58. Relation of regional gray and white matter volumes to current BMI and future increases in BMI: a prospective MRI study. Yokum S, Ng J, Stice E. Int J Obes (Lond) 2012 May; 36 (5): 656-64.

59. Emotional eating and routine restraint scores are associated with activity in brain regions involved in urge and self-control. Wood SM et al. Physiol Behav. 2016 Oct 15; 165: 405-12.

60. Disrupted functional connectivity in adolescent obesity. Moreno-Lopez L et al. Neuroimage Clin. 2016 Jul 12; 12: 262-8.

61. Energy and fructose from beverages sweetened with sugar or high-fructose corn syrup pose a health risk for some people. Bray GA. Adv Nutr. 2013 Mar 1; 4(2): 220-5.

62. Fructose:glucose ratios--a study of sugar self-administration and associated neural and physiological responses in the rat. Levy A et al. Nutrients. 2015 May 22; 7 (5): 3869-90.

63. Differential effects of fructose versus glucose on brain and appetitive responses to food cues and decisions for food rewards. Luo S et al. Proc Natl Acad Sci U S A. 2015 May 19; 112 (20): 6509-14.

64. Physiological handling of dietary fructose-containing sugars: implications for health. Campos VC, Tappy L. Int J Obes (Lond). 2016 Mar; 40 Suppl 1: S6-11. doi: 10.1038/ijo. 2016.8.

65. Fructose, but not glucose, impairs insulin signaling in the three major insulin-sensitive tissues. Baena M et al. Sci Rep. 2016 May 19; 6: 26149.

66. Excess fructose intake-induced hypertrophic visceral adipose tissue results from unbalanced precursor cell adipogenic signals. Zubiría MG et al. FEBS J. 2013 Nov; 280 (22): 5864-74.

67. Relationship between insulin resistance-associated metabolic parameters and anthropometric measurements with sugar-sweetened beverage intake and physical activity levels in US adolescents: findings from the 1999-2004 National Health and Nutrition Examination Survey. Bremer AA, Auinger P, Byrd RS. Arch Pediatr Adolesc Med. 2009 Apr; 163 (4): 328-35.

68. Consuming fructose-sweetened, not glucose-sweetened, beverages increases visceral adiposity and lipids and decreases insulin sensitivity in overweight/obese humans. Stanhope KL et al. J Clin Invest. 2009 May; 119 (5): 1322-34.

69. Greater fructose consumption is associated with cardiometabolic risk markers and visceral adiposity in adolescents. Pollock NK. et al. J Nutr. 2012 Feb; 142 (2): 251-7.

70. Associations among sugar sweetened beverage intake, visceral fat, and cortisol awakening response in minority youth. Shearrer GE et al. Physiol Behav. 2016 Sep 19; 167: 188-193.

71. Sugar-sweetened beverage consumption is associated with change of visceral adipose tissue over 6 years of follow-up. Ma J et al. Circulation. 2016 Jan 26; 133 (4): 370-7. https://www.scientificamerican.com/article/supercharging-brown-fat-to-battle-obesity/

72. Differential role of adipose tissues in obesity and related metabolic and vascular complications. Gómez-Hernández A et al. Int J Endocrinol. 2016; 2016: 1216783.

73. Ng, S.W., Slining, M.M., & Popkin, B.M. (2012). Use of caloric and noncaloric sweeteners in US consumer packaged foods, 2005-2009. Journal of the Academy of Nutrition and Dietetics, 112 (11), 1828-1834. e1821-1826.

74. National Health and Nutrition Examination Survey and the U.S. Department of Agriculture website for information about added sugar guidelines in foods.
See website: https://fnic.nal.usda.gov/sites/fnic.nal.usda.gov/files/uploads/265-338.pdf

75. The truth about sugar: https://youtu.be/9E9bnjwQG9s

76. Dr Robert Lustig at UCSF more detailed information about sugar.
http://www.sugarscience.org/hidden-in-plain-sight/#.WAwEJZMrJUM

77. TED Ed talk: Sugar: Hiding in plain sight by Dr Robert Lustig:
https://youtu.be/Q4CZ81EmAsw

78. The most comprehensive such databases are the USDA Food Composition Databases, at ndb.nal.usda.gov/ndb/.

79. This Wiki website will be of great help to calculate sugar content of foods and drinks: wikihow.com/Count-Your-Sugar-Intake.

80. American Heart Association recommendations for the number of calories from sugar.
http://www.heart.org/HEARTORG/HealthyLiving/HealthyEating/Nutrition/Added-Sugars_UCM_305858_Article.jsp#.WA0XZpMrJUM.

81. The National Heart, Lung, and Blood Institute (NIH)'s "Aim for a Healthy Weight" website offers information on calorie counts per serving in various food, from fruits to fats, at https://healthyeating.nhlbi.nih.gov/.

82. High-intensity interval training versus moderate-intensity continuous training in the prevention/management of cardiovascular disease. Hussain SR et al. Cardiol Rev. 2016 Nov/Dec; 24 (6): 273-28.

83. Exercise training improved body composition, cardiovascular function, and physical fitness of 5-year-old children with obesity or normal body mass. Tan S et al. Pediatr Exerc Sci. 2016 Oct 21: 1-21.

84. Exercise in weight management of obesity. Poirier P, Després JP. Cardiol Clin. 2001 Aug; 19 (3): 459-70.

85. Exercise for health: a randomized, controlled trial evaluating the impact of a pragmatic, translational exercise intervention on the quality of life, function and treatment-related side effects following breast cancer. Hayes SC et al. Breast Cancer Res Treat. 2013 Jan; 137 (1): 175-86.

86. The therapeutic potential of exercise to improve mood, cognition, and sleep in Parkinson's Disease. Reynolds Go et al. Mov Disord. 2016 Jan; 31 (1): 23-38.

87. The effects of exercise on muscle strength, body composition, physical functioning and the inflammatory profile of older adults: a systematic review. Liberman K et al. Curr Opin Clin Nutr Metab Care. 2016 Oct 15.

88. Physical exercise induces hippocampal neurogenesis and prevents cognitive decline. Ma CL et al. Behav Brain Res. 2016 Oct 1; 317: 332-339.

89. The effect of exercise training on resting concentrations of peripheral brain-derived neurotrophic factor (BDNF): A Meta-Analysis. Dinoff A et al. PLoS One. 2016 Sep 22; 11(9): e0163037.

90. Exercise promotes the expression of brain derived neurotrophic factor (BDNF) through the action of the ketone body β-hydroxybutyrate. Sleiman SF et al. Elife. 2016 Jun 2; 5. pii: e15092.

91. Somatosensory brain function and gray matter regional volumes differ according to exercise history: evidence from monozygotic twins. Hautasaari et al. Brain Topogr. 2016 Oct 19. [Epub ahead of print].

92. Exercise: putting action into our epigenome. Denha, J et al. Sports Med. 2014 Feb; 44(2): 189-209.

93. Genetic studies of body mass index yield new insights for obesity biology. Locke AE et al. Nature. 2015 Feb 12; 518 (7538): 197-206.

94. Information about Charles Eugster see: http://www.charleseugster.net/home.

95. Reducing occupational sitting time and improving worker health: The take-a-stand project, 2011. Pronk et al. https://www.cdc.gov/pcd/issues/2012/11_0323.htm. Lancet. 2016 Sep 24; 388 (10051): 1302-10.

96. All-cause mortality attributable to sitting time: Analysis of 54 countries worldwide. Leandro Fórnias Machado Rezende et al. American Journal of Preventative medicine. 2016 Aug 51; 2: (253-263).

97. Does physical activity attenuate, or even eliminate, the detrimental association of sitting time with mortality? A harmonised meta-analysis of data from more than 1 million men and women. Ekelund U et al. Lancet. 2016 Sep 24; 388 (10051): 1302-10.

98. Exercise regulation of adipose tissue. Stanford KI, Goodyear LJ. Adipocyte. 2016 May 18; 5 (2): 153-62.

99. Impact of endurance exercise training on adipocyte microRNA expression in overweight men. Tsiloulis T et al. FASEB J. 2016 Sep 28. pii: fj.201600678R. [Epub ahead of print].

100. Do activity monitors increase physical activity in adults with overweight or obesity? A systematic review and meta-analysis. De Vries HJ et al. Obesity (Silver Spring). 2016 Oct; 24 (10): 2078-91. doi: 10.1002/oby.21619.

101. Effect of wearable technology combined with a lifestyle intervention on long-term weight loss: The IDEA randomized clinical crial.Jakicic et al. JAMA. 2016 Sep 20; 316 (11): 1161-1171.

102. The role of dopamine in positive and negative prediction error utilization during incidental learning - Insights from Positron Emission Tomography, Parkinson's disease and Huntington's disease. Mathar et al. Cortex. 2016 Sep 19. pii: S0010-9452 (16) 30240-4.

ABOUT THE AUTHOR

Dr. Selena Bartlett studied mathematics and then followed in her father's footsteps by completing a pharmacy degree in 1989 and becoming a pharmacist in her native Australia. Her life took another direction when her sister was hospitalized with mental-health problems. The impact this had on both her sister and their family led Selena to realize how little we knew about the brain. She completed her Ph.D. in neuropharmacology in 1995. She continued studying the brain for the next twenty-five years, first with a postdoctoral fellowship in neuroscience at the John Curtin School of Medical Research, in Canberra, Australia.

From 2004 to 2012, Selena directed the Preclinical Development Group at the Ernest Gallo Clinic and Research Center, a top alcohol- and addiction-research institution, at the University of California at San Francisco. Here she focused on turning basic research discoveries into treatments for neurological problems such as addiction, pain, stress, anxiety, and depression. Selena is now a group leader in addiction neuroscience and obesity at the Translational Research Institute at the Institute of Health and Biomedical Innovation, as well as a research capacity building professor in the School of Clinical Sciences, Faculty of Health and Behavioural Sciences, at the Queensland University of Technology. In 2014 she presented her findings on brain fitness and the neuroplasticity revolution in a TEDx Talk. An ambassador for the organization Women in Technology, Selena received the organization's Biotech Outstanding Achievement and Biotech Research awards in 2013. She has written more than eighty scientific papers and presented her findings to many government institutions, companies, institutions, high schools, and community organizations.

Selena presents lectures and seminars, and has designed programs to help government, business, and other organizations improve innovation, decision making, and performance; aid children in learning; assist women and men in strengthening brain health to trim the body; and help retirees in having more vital lives. Her most-requested speaking topics are on how to manage stress to grow mindset, embrace change, and trim the body; growing leadership mindset; improving team performance; and how adverse childhood experiences shape the brain and what to do about it. Believing this work has the potential to be transformative, even to disrupt the cycle of trauma, poverty, and incarceration, she is a passionate advocate for people who are marginalized. Selena understands that knowing one's brain drives compassion for other brains.

This book is the culmination of her efforts to help people understand the importance of the brain's plasticity and apply practical neuroscience tools to their lives.

A portion of the proceeds from this book will be donated to the Francesca Foundation, dedicated to raising awareness about the brain to improve the lives of children.

ACKNOWLEDGMENTS

I want to start by applauding the great scientists and professionals working tirelessly to understand the brain and help people improve their lives—in particular, the many people who contributed their knowledge and support to my research and scientific and personal development.

I would like to thank the many people who offered their personal insights to improve and shape my work into an approachable and practical neuroscience book. My thanks to Sheryl Batchelor, Lincoln Jay, and Anna Tarraran. I appreciate the support of my research team, who continue the painstaking work of unraveling the mysteries of the brain to benefit people suffering debilitating brain disorders.

I could not have produced *Smashing Mindset* without Patty Harper and Khaldoun Tayyeb, who helped with the content and design; editors Jillian Corey and Pamela Feinsilber, who made it read better; illustrator Jane Mjolsness, who made it look better; and Thrive Publishing.

Thank you to my sister Nina Wines and great friends Susan and Rob Allen, and to my friends on either side of the Pacific Ocean, for believing in and supporting me through the great and not so great times. Thanks to my parents, June and Francis, and to my brother, Damien, and our extended families and loved ones for their support.

And a special thanks to my beautiful children, James and Ella, for putting up with my obsession with working out how to help people understand their brains, since it has taken time away from you. I am forever grateful.

CONTACTS

To learn more about Smashing Mindset
or to organize an event or a workshop:

www.smashmindset.com and
sbartlett@smashmindset.com
email: info@miggimatters.com
website: www.miggimatters.com
facebook.com/miggimatters
twitter.com/miggimatters
instagram.com/miggimatters
pinterest.com/miggimatters

MIGGI MATTERS – 1st edition prior to this latest Smashing Mindset edition

Visit our website: www.miggimatters.com
or Email: info@miggimatters.com

TESTIMONIALS

This book is an amazing read, particularly the chapter about will power. In five well written chapters Dr Selena Bartlett suggests ways how to shed unhealthy habits and how to train our consciousness for lasting improvement of our physical and mental state. It is key to live truly happier, better lives.

Iris Assing, Kenilworth, U.K.

With Selena's help I retrained my brain to over-ride my amygdala which occasionally threatened to ignite my fight and flight response bringing panic before a presentation. I regularly thank and acknowledge Selena in my coaching programs, sharing stories about the brain's plasticity, power poses and positive affirmations and how understanding these concepts can make you be a better presenter and communicator. Selena explained why and how my home-spun tips and techniques worked by sharing her knowledge of the brain and how it functions.

Helen Besly, Managing Director, Rowland, Brisbane, Australia.

Dr. Bartlett gave me the confidence I needed to make significant changes in my life. Her dedicated efforts as a neuroscientist and firm understanding of how the brain works provided me the link that I had always been searching for — explaining the "Whys" of so many common diet tips. Armed with a new clear grasp of what I needed to do and how, and with her positive, helpful scientific approach I have been able to move forward with confidence and success. I recommend to anyone wanting change in their life to allow them selves to be guided by the research, teachings and science-based approach Dr. Bartlett provides.

Ira Kargel, CEO and President, Gears Bike Shop, Toronto, Canada.

I am a cancer survivor and take tamoxifen as post treatment to secure the odds that the cancer won't come back. I was surprised to discover that the exercises in *MiGGi Matters (1st Ed)* helped me coach my brain to manage stress which helped me sleep better. Who would have ever thought that you could train the MiGGi monster to help with insomnia! I truly feel that brain training could help anyone. I highly recommend reading *MiGGi Matters* and doing the easy exercises.

Robin, mother, professional dancer, entrepreneur, Berkeley, California.

Selena Bartlett has a wealth of knowledge about resilience and the inner workings of the brain. Her years of experience as a neuroscientist allow her to leverage this knowledge for the layperson. My experience of her presentation that I attended two years ago was to walk away with my eyes open and questions percolating. The information I gleaned has allowed me to continue to look at my life and that of my family's through a different lens.

Christine Mattson, Senior Partner, Hilburn, Berkeley, California

I just wanted to take the time to thank you for being an inspiration in my adapting new Life Style Behaviours after attending a lecture you gave and reading your book. Your passion and role modelling together with scientific research helped me on my journey to a happy & healthier life. I have used many of your strategies and words of wisdom to assist me with previous unhealthy lifestyle choices. I saw my doctor the other day and the 22 kg weight loss I have had over the last 18 months has seen my pathology return to within normal ranges and most importantly a decrease in my BGL. I am still on this new path but know I will succeed to achieve my goals and make this new lifestyle just that my normal lifestyle and not a series of fad diets that don't work.

Joanne Cupples, Lecturer, Queensland University of Technology, Brisbane, Australia.

I had trichotillomania for 35 years. I didn't know that's what it was. I didn't actually pull my hair out, but constantly 'played' with it, searching for hairs of certain textures then fiddling with them. This was usually when I was watching TV, reading or driving. When my daughter developed severe mental health disorders including Obsessive Compulsive Disorder, I discovered that I had a (milder) form of trichotillomania – which happens to be a variant of OCD and anxiety disorder. The trichotillomania was out of control while my daughter was very ill. My arms were up to my head so much I had arm pain.

Professor Selena Bartlett is a dear friend of mine from school days. We re-established contact through social media a few years ago. I haven't seen her for many years but in a show of support for her amazing and ground breaking work I bought a copy of *Miggi Matters*. I didn't really know what I was buying but this book was a God send. For me the most valuable thing I learnt was recognising that my hair pulling was my way of dealing with stress – my amygdala would go into fight or flight mode and I would pull at my hair. Recognising my hair pulling as a '**Miggi moment**' helped me re-direct my stress to less harmful behaviours. The tracing was invaluable and if I didn't have access to pencil and paper I would trace the seams in my clothes. Within four weeks my hair pulling had stopped. I now rarely go to pull my hair and when I do I can say to myself 'Oh this is a Miggi Moment' take a few deep breaths and that's it.

Thank you Selena for never giving up on unravelling the mysteries of our brain and providing user friendly strategies to help eliminate harmful behaviours. I'm awaiting you next book with much anticipation.

Therese Groen, speech pathologist, Perth, Western Australia.

This book was a game changer for me! We all "know" what we need to be doing in regards to diet and exercise but Selena explains how to train your brain to work with you, not against you and she does this in an easy to read style. If you struggle with sugar addiction this book is a must read.

Anna Tarraran, Teacher, Education Support, Queensland, Australia.

I would thoroughly recommend the groundbreaking research that focuses on the principles of neuroplasticity to support children to overcome the cognitive and emotional impact of significant disadvantage and trauma by improving their executive function skills. The outcomes for the children and young people on the trial were amazing and to see the way children were able to build their understanding of their own brain function and in turn create new pathways of behaviour was extremely rewarded and exceeded our hopes for the young people.

Rob Ryan, Managing Director, Key Assets, Australasia region.

Many of our staff have purchased Selena's book because they now understand the power of the Amygdala and can override automated responses of the brain to improve impulse control. QUT staff attend Selena's seminars because she is passionate, authentic and possesses the ability to transfer expertise into layperson's language. Professor Bartlett has, over several years, delivered engaging and innovative seminars to improve literacy about mental health, neurological function and how understanding the brain and body systems can empower choices and behaviours.

Ms Deborah Ward-Mackay, Senior wellness co-ordinator,
Queensland University of Technology, Brisbane, Australia.

The underpinning narrative of Professor Bartlett's work is to revolutionise the way society understands and deals with brain health. Professor Bartlett is a charismatic, engaging and knowledgeable. Complex neurological concepts are communicated to the audience in simple to understand language and examples. Professor Bartlett's enthusiasm and passion is inspiring. I highly recommend her book.

Steven Jonsson – Senior Team Leader in Statutory Child Protection Investigations; and Sessional Academic QUT, Brisbane, Australia.

What people are saying on Amazon. 100% rating with 5 stars from all reviews.

This book really helped! A thoughtful, short and sweet book with strategies that are easy to follow — I loved this book. I really felt the author's intention to inspire her readers with excellent, real-world examples and insights to help us manage the inevitable stresses that make up our daily lives. I've had this book for a few months now, although I've been loaning it out to friends who now are experiencing similar positive, life-changing "aha moments."

Joss K.

Fantastic easy to read book that outlines the importance of understanding your brain. Would highly recommend it to anyone who needs some guidance in making a change to their life.

Sheryl Batchelor, Director, Stronger Brains, CEO, Brain Fitness Coaching, Brisbane, Australia.

Yes, it's not a cliche: you can change your thinking and it will help you to change your life. Thank you, Dr. Selena Bartlett, for explaining to us these invaluable concepts of brain fitness and the neuroplasticity revolution. Truly inspiring. Loved this book — easy read with fun but educational activities!

A Don.

Turns out — you have to change your brain to change your life. I had never really thought about how the wiring of my physical brain impacted my impulses, choices and thought patterns. Great to know that I can actually re-wire my brain to change things for the better. It makes so much sense, now that I get it. Very easy to understand language and visuals and simple, daily activities make this book super helpful and truly a way to make positive change in your life. So glad that I found this very approachable and valuable neuroscience.

By mookitabanana.

This was a gamechanger for me, how the brain works explained in everyday language by a neuroscientist for everyday people. The simple powerful practical steps have changed my life in how I now slow my mind down to handle stress. I have quietened the 'Miggi monster' by training my brain to lock onto positive rather than negative, and understanding negative is the brains natural default- it's not my fault! Highly recommended.

By Amazon Customer.

Great manual for healthy minds and bodies!
This is necessary knowledge for all ages! The book is a quick and easy read, but the lessons are critical to a healthy mind and body. Dr. Bartlett has distilled the core ideas from current research on exercise, diet and neuroplasticity and presented them in a form easily digestible for all ages and backgrounds. I highly recommend it.

By Amazon Customer.

Great book with practical tips for taming everyday stress! A well-written, easy to read book full of practical advice. The idea of having a 'MiGGi moment' — and being able to manage them — has had a significant impact on my work and home life. The tracing exercises really work! I would recommend this book to anyone who wants to get the upper hand on managing their stress.

By Amazon Customer.

CPSIA information can be obtained
at www.ICGtesting.com
Printed in the USA
BVHW031029190822
645004BV00012B/194